LabVIEW Graphical Programming Cookbook

69 recipes to help you build, debug, and deploy
modular applications using LabVIEW

Yik Yang

[PACKT] enterprise 𝕏
PUBLISHING   professional expertise distilled

BIRMINGHAM - MUMBAI

LabVIEW Graphical Programming Cookbook

First published: January 2014

Production Reference: 1160114

Published by Packt Publishing Ltd.
Livery Place
35 Livery Street
Birmingham B3 2PB, UK.

ISBN 978-1-78217-140-9

www.packtpub.com

Cover Image by Zarko Piljak (zpiljak@gmail.com)

Credits

Author
Yik Yang

Reviewers
Amit Dongol
Chris Larson
Qizhen Ruan
Justin Smith

Acquisition Editor
Rubal Kaur

Lead Technical Editors
Madhuja Chaudhari
Mandar Ghate

Technical Editors
Tanvi Bhatt
Dipika Gaonkar
Monica John
Neha Mankare

Copy Editors
Sayanee Mukherjee
Lavina Pereira

Project Coordinator
Venitha Cutinho

Proofreader
Amy Johnson

Indexer
Mehreen Deshmukh

Production Coordinator
Conidon Miranda

Cover Work
Conidon Miranda

About the Author

Yik Yang is a test engineer living in Chicago who has specialized in automation and data analysis. Having worked in multiple fields such as semiconductor, automotive, and power, he has experience with different types of automation and understands what are the industries' needs.

He started his career after receiving his Bachelor's and Master's degrees in Electrical Engineering at Virginia Tech. In his career, he worked on automation projects that used CompactDAQ, PXI, FPGA, and so on in LabVIEW. He has also spent a lot of time with Lean Six Sigma and statistical analysis with JMP. He is a certified Professional Engineer (PE) in North Carolina and a Certified LabVIEW Developer (CLD).

I would like to thank my wife Qian and my son Elijah. They have given me a tremendous amount of love and support in the process of finishing this book. Most importantly, I would like to thank God, as without him I would not be alive and capable of writing this book after my terrifying bicycle accident, when I was directly hit by a truck.

About the Reviewers

Amit Dongol is a Ph.D candidate (Physics). He is working on setting up a research lab with LabVIEW interface for data acquisition.

Chris Larson has been using LabVIEW for nine years. Currently he is working as a researcher and developer of cloud-based functionality for LabVIEW. He is an expert at developing systems that take advantage of the connected world and Internet.

Chris learned LabVIEW while working at 3M's SEMS Research and Development lab. While at 3M, he created numerous LabVIEW-based systems to develop and manufacture products for 3M's divisions including safety and security, display and graphics, and health care. His contributions include antenna designs for RFID file tracking, improved manufacturing of retro-reflective materials, improved quality control for display brightening films, and improved high-speed manufacturing of specialty medical tapes.

Qizhen Ruan is a software engineer. He has over 13 years of experience in LabVIEW development. He has designed and developed many LabVIEW features.

Justin Smith has a degree in Computer Science from Tennessee Technological University, and is currently a Systems and Solutions Integrator for an industrial IT firm in Nashville, Tennessee. He develops core software for interfacing with third-party hardware and software and has recently introduced this software as modules in LabVIEW. Primarily a Java developer, Justin has been using open source tools to allow the code to be run from within LabVIEW.

Having grown up around computers in the '80s, Justin had always known that he wanted to pursue a career in computing. After working as an intern in college and spending over a year in Central Mexico for his company, he realized all the good that can be done by helping to improve industrial processes (safety, quality, efficiency). This made him decide that he wanted to continue working in a industrial IT and automation. He also felt that the manufacturing industry has yet to see the same technological revolutions as other business sectors through the advances of companies such as Facebook and Google.

Justin has been working for Summit Management Systems, Inc of Nashville Tennessee for nearly 10 years. Celebrating its 20th anniversary in business, Summit Management Systems offers custom integration and process solutions worldwide for the industrial and manufacturing sector as well as several stand-alone software packages that aid in data acquisition from industrial devices and software for manufacturing workflow management systems.

I would like to thank my father for all the opportunities that he has given me to make me who I am. From allowing me to grow up around computers to encouraging me to enter the software development field, he is the reason I was able to work on this book and review it. Thanks Dad.

---

www.PacktPub.com

Support files, eBooks, discount offers and more

You might want to visit www.PacktPub.com for support files and downloads related to your book.

Did you know that Packt offers eBook versions of every book published, with PDF and ePub files available? You can upgrade to the eBook version at www.PacktPub.com and as a print book customer, you are entitled to a discount on the eBook copy. Get in touch with us at service@packtpub.com for more details.

At www.PacktPub.com, you can also read a collection of free technical articles, sign up for a range of free newsletters and receive exclusive discounts and offers on Packt books and eBooks.

http://PacktLib.PacktPub.com

Do you need instant solutions to your IT questions? PacktLib is Packt's online digital book library. Here, you can access, read and search across Packt's entire library of books.

Why Subscribe?

- ▸ Fully searchable across every book published by Packt
- ▸ Copy and paste, print and bookmark content
- ▸ On demand and accessible via web browser

Free Access for Packt account holders

If you have an account with Packt at www.PacktPub.com, you can use this to access PacktLib today and view nine entirely free books. Simply use your login credentials for immediate access.

Table of Contents

Preface

LabVIEW is a graphical programming language by National Instrument. Mainly, it is used in test and automation fields for instrument control, data acquisition, and so on. In this book, we will cover different areas in LabVIEW programming with practical examples that follow sound coding standard and design rules.

What this book covers

Chapter 1, *Understanding the LabVIEW Environment*, covers common settings and functions in the LabVIEW environment.

Chapter 2, *Customizing the User Interface*, covers different functions used in creating an UI.

Chapter 3, *Working with Common Architectures*, covers common architectures in LabVIEW.

Chapter 4, *Managing Data*, covers how to use memory efficiently and control the data flow.

Chapter 5, *Passing Data*, covers different methods of passing data.

Chapter 6, *Error Handling*, covers different methods of error handling.

Chapter 7, *Working with Files*, covers how to work with different file types.

Chapter 8, *Understanding Data Acquisition*, covers acquiring data with different types of instruments.

Chapter 9, *Simplifying Code*, covers ways to simplify code.

Chapter 10, *Working with External Code and Applications*, covers how to use external code and application within LabVIEW.

What you need for this book

The examples in this chapter are written in the LabVIEW 2012 development environment, but they also work in LabVIEW 2013. The development environment comes in different packages. The highest package is the developer suite. Some examples in this book require toolkits included in the developer suite. It is more economical to buy the developer suite than to buy the toolkits individually. To purchase the developer suite, visit www.ni.com.

Who this book is for

The book is intended for readers who know the basic features of LabVIEW to advanced LabVIEW programmers.

Conventions

In this book, you will find a number of styles of text that distinguish between different kinds of information. Here are some examples of these styles, and an explanation of their meaning.

Code words in text, database table names, folder names, filenames, file extensions, pathnames, dummy URLs, user input, and Twitter handles are shown as follows: " Create the main VI that calls Coordinates.vi."

New terms and **important words** are shown in bold. Words that you see on the screen, in menus or dialog boxes for example, appear in the text like this: " Right-click on the picture ring and select **Add Item**."

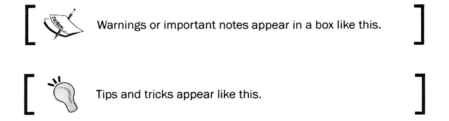

Warnings or important notes appear in a box like this.

Tips and tricks appear like this.

Reader feedback

Feedback from our readers is always welcome. Let us know what you think about this book—what you liked or may have disliked. Reader feedback is important for us to develop titles that you really get the most out of.

To send us general feedback, simply send an e-mail to feedback@packtpub.com, and mention the book title via the subject of your message.

If there is a topic that you have expertise in and you are interested in either writing or contributing to a book, see our author guide on www.packtpub.com/authors.

Customer support

Now that you are the proud owner of a Packt book, we have a number of things to help you to get the most from your purchase.

Errata

Although we have taken every care to ensure the accuracy of our content, mistakes do happen. If you find a mistake in one of our books—maybe a mistake in the text or the code—we would be grateful if you would report this to us. By doing so, you can save other readers from frustration and help us improve subsequent versions of this book. If you find any errata, please report them by visiting http://www.packtpub.com/submit-errata, selecting your book, clicking on the **errata submission form** link, and entering the details of your errata. Once your errata are verified, your submission will be accepted and the errata will be uploaded on our website, or added to any list of existing errata, under the Errata section of that title. Any existing errata can be viewed by selecting your title from http://www.packtpub.com/support.

Piracy

Piracy of copyright material on the Internet is an ongoing problem across all media. At Packt, we take the protection of our copyright and licenses very seriously. If you come across any illegal copies of our works, in any form, on the Internet, please provide us with the location address or website name immediately so that we can pursue a remedy.

Please contact us at copyright@packtpub.com with a link to the suspected pirated material.

We appreciate your help in protecting our authors, and our ability to bring you valuable content.

Questions

You can contact us at questions@packtpub.com if you are having a problem with any aspect of the book, and we will do our best to address it.

1

Understanding the LabVIEW Environment

In this chapter, we will cover:

- ▸ Configuring essentials
- ▸ Configuring quick drop
- ▸ Using debug tools
- ▸ Creating custom probe
- ▸ Compiling EXE
- ▸ Debugging EXE
- ▸ Compiling a standalone application

Introduction

This chapter explains how to configure LabVIEW and how to use its functions. The first two recipes explain how to configure commonly-encountered settings, and the remaining recipes explain how to use common functions in LabVIEW.

Configuring essentials

Before using LabVIEW, it is important to set up the environment for maximum productivity. There are a lot of settings in LabVIEW. We do not need to configure everything; the default setting would usually suffice. However, we should at least configure the layout of the **Controls** palette, the layout of the **Functions** palette, and the LabVIEW option, before we start coding.

How to do it...

We will start by configuring the **Functions** palette. Configuring the **Controls** palette is not shown, but it is similar to configuring the **Functions** palette. Here are the steps to configure the **Functions** palette:

1. To configure the **Functions** palette, right-click on the block diagram to get the palette and left-click on the thumb pin to pin it down. On the palette, navigate to **Customize | View this Palette As**, and select your preference on how the palette should be arranged. For this example, select **Category (Icons and Text)**.

2. In **Customize**, select **Change Visible Palettes...**, and then select which categories should appear on the palette. Only the categories that are used frequently should be selected. The unselected categories are still accessible by clicking on the double arrow (pointed down) at the bottom of the palette. The following screenshot shows the **Functions** palette pinned downed, with the **Customize** menu activated:

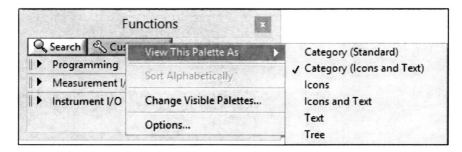

3. Only the first category of the palette will stay open, so the category that is used the most (**Programming**) should be at the top. When the palette is pinned down, there is a pair of parallel lines (**‖**) on the left of each category (left of right arrow). The parallel lines are used to move the categories. The following screenshot shows how the **Functions** palette looks like after the configuration:

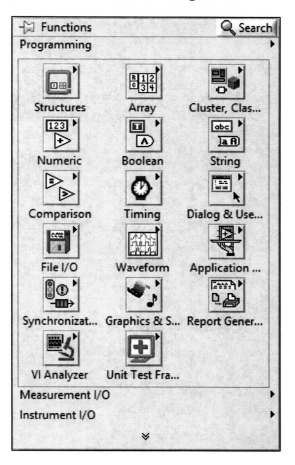

4. In the LabVIEW option, we can configure the LabVIEW environment in detail. The readability and space utilization can be improved. In the block diagram, click on **Tools** and **Options**. Under the **Block Diagram** category, deselect the **Place front panel terminals as icons** to save space on the block diagram, and then select **Use transparent name labels** for a cleaner block diagram. The size of controls and indicators are reduced in the block diagram, and the name labels look cleaner in the block diagram compared to the name labels that are opaque. The following screenshot shows the LabVIEW option dialog:

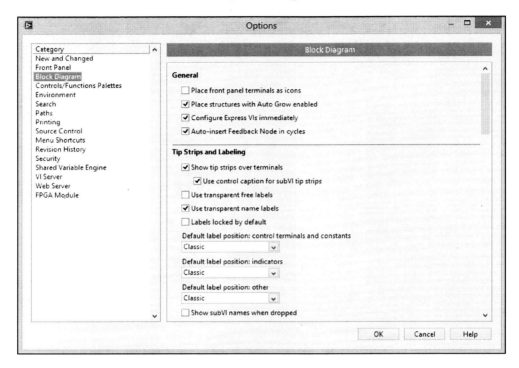

How it works...

The palette settings and LabVIEW options are not saved locally in the **VI** (**Virtual Instrument**) file that contains both the block diagram and front panel. They are saved globally, so every time a new VI is created, the saved settings and options would apply. Inside the LabVIEW installation folder, a file called LabVIEW.ini resides. The file contains all the saved settings and options and is loaded when LabVIEW starts. If we wish to transfer the settings from one computer to another, we can save this file and transfer it to the same location in the other computer.

For both the **Controls** and **Functions** palette, only what are necessary should be on them, and the rest should be hidden. The **Controls** palette is for the front panel, and the **Functions** palette is for the block diagram. We will only demonstrate how to set up the **Functions** palette, but keep in mind that the same procedures apply for setting up the **Controls** palette.

Configuring quick drop

The **quick drop** feature was introduced in LabVIEW 8.6. Previously, finding a function would require navigating and searching through the palette. With quick drop, finding a function can be done through a text-based search without going through the palette. To do a search, the name of the function is entered and, as it is entered, a list of possible functions would appear for the user to choose. To make searching easier, a function can be associated with a keyboard shortcut, and to make quick drop even more amazing, repetitive tasks can be associated with a keyboard shortcut.

How to do it...

We will start by associating the while loop function with a keyboard shortcut. Here are the steps to do that:

1. Press *Ctrl* + spacebar to invoke quick drop and click on **Shortcut**. As an example, we will associate shortcut *W* + *L* to the while loop. Under **Diagram Shortcut**, enter **wl**. Under **Diagram Shortcut Object**, enter **While Loop**. If we are unsure about the name of the function, we can always find the function inside the palette and look for its name. Finally, we click on **Add** and then on **OK** to add the customized shortcut into the quick drop configuration. The following screenshot shows how the shortcut is added:

Besides finding functions quickly, we can assign a shortcut to a plugin that accomplishes predefined tasks.

2. To execute a plugin via shortcut, we press *Ctrl* + Space and the shortcut of the plugin. Built-in shortcuts are available for routine tasks. The following are a few examples of built-in shortcuts:

    ❑ *Ctrl + Space* and then *Ctrl + D* creates all controls and indicators for a **subVI**

    ❑ *Ctrl + Space* and then *Ctrl + R* deletes a subVI, while also cleaning up all unnecessary wires and re-connecting broken ones

    ❑ *Ctrl + Space* and then *Ctrl + T* moves the labels of all controls and indicators to their left and right

    If built-in plugins are not adequate, we can customize our own plugin and assign a shortcut to it.

3. To make a plugin, use the template in `LabVIEW\resource\dialog\ QuickDrop\QuickDrop Plugin Template.vi` as a starting point. After the plugin is completed, it needs to be placed within `LabVIEW\resource\dialog\ QuickDrop\plugins` or `LabVIEW Data\Quick Drop Plugins`. If the plugin is placed within the `LabVIEW` folder, it will only be available to that version of LabVIEW. If the plugin is placed into the other path, versions of LabVIEW from 2010 and up can use the plugin. Follow the previous step to assign a shortcut to a plugin.

How it works...

When a shortcut is associated with a function or a task, the shortcut is saved in the LabVIEW configuration so that it can be used again.

See also

▶ For useful plugins that are made by other LabVIEW users, please visit the link `https://decibel.ni.com/content/groups/quick-drop-enthusiasts?view=documents`.

Using debug tools

Many features exist in LabVIEW for debugging a program. Text-based programmers should already be familiar with some of the features, such as step in, step out, and so on, but there are some features that may sound unfamiliar.

How to do it...

Before jumping into the code, let's check the obvious:

1. Examine the run button (a right arrow) on the block diagram to see if it is broken or not. If it is broken, click on it to see a list of problems that we must fix. If we double-click on an item of the list, LabVIEW will bring us to the location of the problem. We need to fix all the problems first before we can go further. To see what a broken arrow looks like, open a new VI and place an add node under the **Numeric** palette to it. Click on the broken arrow to see what the cause of the broken arrow is.

2. After the run arrow turns solid, we can start debugging the program. First, we turn on **Retain Wire Values** by clicking on its button on the block diagram toolbar. This will enable us to examine the values in all the wires. Then we navigate to the location of interest and set a breakpoint by right-clicking on the location, selecting Breakpoint, and **Set Breakpoint**.

3. After we set up the program for debugging, click on the run arrow to run the program. The program will pause at the breakpoint. If we placed our breakpoint on a SubVI, we can choose to step over it, so that we stay on our current VI without going deeper; or we can step into it, so that we go into the subVI for further investigation. If we are already in a subVI and we want to get out, we can step out of it. To step into, step over, or step out, we can click on the corresponding button on the block diagram toolbar. The following screenshot shows the portion of the block diagram toolbar discussed:

4. To examine the value of a wire, right-click on the wire and select **Probe**. A dialog will pop up and show the wire's value. When the program has not sent data through that wire, the value is not populated. Once the value is populated, it will show up in the dialog. With the probe, we can view the data within the wire, but we cannot modify it.

5. To activate **Highlight Execution**, we click on its button on the block diagram toolbar. This feature allows us to view how the data is actually flowing in the program, but our program will slow down. Many LabVIEW programmers find this useful because it allows them to grasp how the data flows in a VI.

 Be careful when you use this feature. Since it slows down the program, it may create bugs that are timing-related.

How it works...

Debugging tools allow programmers to look at a program in depth by offering features to control the flow of the program.

Creating custom probe

Custom probe is an enhancement to the generic probe which only allows users to examine the value of a wire. A custom probe is able to pause the program using conditional statements inside the probe. By doing that, the custom probe acts like a conditional breakpoint. Also, it can process and extract information from the raw data to facilitate the debugging process.

How to do it...

We will create a custom probe with a VI that is built-in to LabVIEW installation. The following are the steps to do that:

1. We will use the code shown in the following screenshot to set up the custom probe. The code contains an outer while loop that executes the inner for loop continuously. The inner for loop would generate an array of 0 to 10 elements randomly, and each element would contain a random number between 0 to 30. In this example, we want the execution to pause when the array generation contains more than 9 elements.

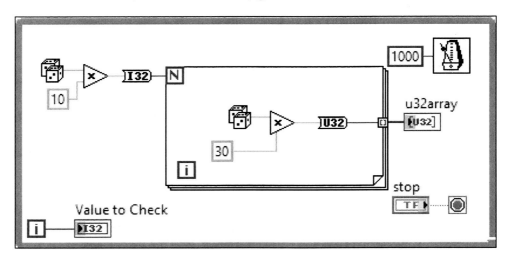

2. To create a custom probe, right-click on the wire feeding the U32 array indicator and navigate to **Custom Probe | New**. When a dialog appears, select **Create a probe from an existing probe** and click on **Next**. A dialog with a list of probes would appear. From the list, in our example, we select the **Conditional Unsigned32 Array Probe**. When a probe is selected, a detailed description about the probe is shown below the list. This is how we determine whether an existing probe is suitable for our application or not. When we click on **Next**, the next page appears, and we enter u32array as **Filename** and leave all other options at the default setting. We click on **Save**. See the following screenshot to initiate the setup:

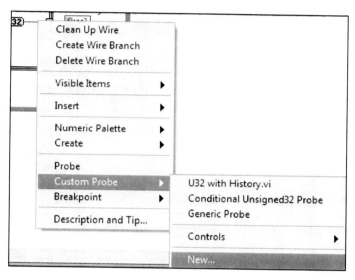

3. We have created a custom probe for our application based on an existing one from the LabVIEW installation. To try out the custom probe, we right-click on the wire feeding the U32 array indicator and select **Custom Probe** | u32array.vi. The **Probe Watch Window** appears; on the right side, it contains a tab control with two tabs. The first tab shows the data and the size of the array. The size of the array is a function for this custom probe. It is not present in a generic probe. The second tab contains all the conditions that we can set to stop the execution of the program. For our example, we will set the check box to make **Number of element** as the criterion, and set the criteria to greater than nine. After we finish the custom probe setup, we click on the run button to start the program. Since we put a Wait Until Next ms Multiple node and set it at equal to 1000ms, the outer while loop will iterate once every second. While the program is running, we can go to **Probe Watch Window** and look at the data. Once the criterion is met, the program would pause, and we can probe other wires on the block diagram if we want to.

How it works...

When we created a custom probe based on an existing probe, we can use the probes located in the `vi.lib` folder of the LabVIEW installation folder. To use a custom probe, we should save the probe in the `\default` folder located at `<LabVIEW>\user.lib\_probes` or the `Probes` folder located at `<Documents>\LabVIEW Data\`. If the probe is saved in the first path (the `default` folder), LabVIEW will use that custom probe as the default probe for that particular data type.

Compiling EXE

The machine where we will deploy our code usually does not have LabVIEW development software. To deploy our code, we need to install LabVIEW run time engine with the correct version (free of charge), and deploy an executable instead of deploying a set of VI.

How to do it...

Before compiling an executable, we will create a project that contains both the VI and the executable that is built from the VI. Here are the steps for creating a project:

1. To create a project, the easiest way is to select **Create Project** and then **Blank Project** at the startup screen. Or, if we already have a VI, we can select **Project | Create Project | Blank Project**. Within the project, right-click on **My Computer** and select **New | VI**. Now the VI is within the project, we will create a VI called `EXEvi.vi` to calculate a 1 cycle sinusoidal waveform with given amplitude, phase, and frequency. It contains an event structure with an event case that will execute when the **Read File** Boolean control is clicked. See the following screenshot for the example:

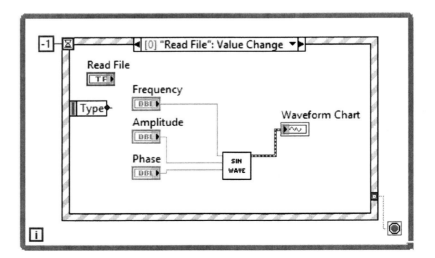

2. The subVI, **SinWave.vi**, in the preceding example takes the input parameters to calculate the sampling rate and number of samples for one cycle of waveform before using the Sine Waveform.vi to generate the waveform. Refer to *Chapter 3, Working with Common Architectures* for creating a subVI. See the following screenshot:

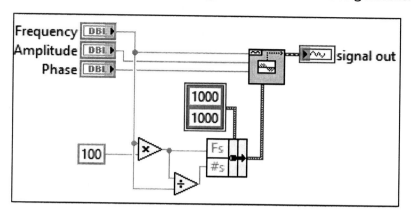

3. To compile the executable, right-click on **Build Specifications** and select **New | Application (EXE)** within the project. The **My Application Properties** dialog will pop up and we will set up each category of the dialog. In the Information category, we enter ExeExampleBuild under the **Build Specifications** name. That name would appear under Build Specification within our project. We enter ExeExample.exe under the Target filename, and that is the actual name of the executable. For the Destination directory, enter a convenient location for development.

4. In the Source Files category, select **EXEvi.vi**, and click on the right arrow next to Startup VIs so that the VI will appear when the executable is invoked. As for Always Included, if the program calls VI dynamically or by reference, works with files, and so on, we can include these dependencies that the program uses. Since the subVI, **SinWave.vi**, is part of the program, the compiler knows that it needs to include the subVI in the compilation without specification.

5. Under Destinations, we will leave everything as default. If we have dependencies (subVIs, files, and so on), we can choose where to place them relative to the executable. The dependencies can either go into the executable or into a support directory. We can add additional destinations if we so desire. In this category, we are configuring all the destinations where the files can go.

6. Under **Source File Settings**, we can choose how the files are included with the executable. If we click on **EXEvi.vi**, we see that **Inclusion Type** is **Startup VI**, since we have already specified the same under the **Source Files** category. The destination of **Startup VI** is the executable itself, which means the **Startup VI** is not located at `...\ExeExample.exe\EXEvi.vi`. For **SinWave.vi**, we will use the default setting. The default setting will put the subVI inside the executable as well. The following screenshot shows how the project looks like with executable:

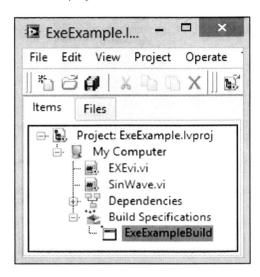

How it works...

For an executable to run on a computer, it must at least have LabVIEW runtime engine with the correct version. Some other device drivers may be required as well. We will discuss this topic in the *Compiling a standalone application* recipe in this chapter.

Debugging EXE

Sometimes, our code will work perfectly in the development environment, but will fail miserably when we deploy and run its executable on another computer. When that happens, we can put more indicators into the VI to display data at relevant locations of the program. Then, we can re-compile the executable and use the extra data to find the bug. If that still does not work, we can step through the executable similar to what we do in the development environment.

How to do it...

If our code works perfectly in development, but fails miserably after deployment in the executable mode, how do we debug the executable?

1. We do not have the LabVIEW development software on the machine where we deploy the executable, so how do we step through the executable? We will connect to the machine where the EXE is deployed (EXE machine) from another computer that has the LabVIEW development software installed (DEV machine). The two computers must be on the same network; we verify their connection by issuing the `ping` command in the command prompt with the EXE machine's IP address from the DEV computer. See following screenshot for an example:

```
C:\Users\yangy>ping 192.168.0.195

Pinging 192.168.0.195 with 32 bytes of data:
Reply from 192.168.0.195: bytes=32 time=355ms TTL=128
Reply from 192.168.0.195: bytes=32 time=1ms TTL=128
Reply from 192.168.0.195: bytes=32 time=1ms TTL=128
Reply from 192.168.0.195: bytes=32 time=1ms TTL=128

Ping statistics for 192.168.0.195:
    Packets: Sent = 4, Received = 4, Lost = 0 (0% loss),
Approximate round trip times in milli-seconds:
    Minimum = 1ms, Maximum = 355ms, Average = 89ms
```

2. After we verify that we can ping the EXE machine from the DEV machine, we need to recompile the executable with **Enable debugging option** selected, so that the block diagram is compiled into the executable for debugging purposes. The option is inside executable properties and under the Advanced category. Within **Enable debugging option**, there is another option that we can select; it is **Wait for debugger on launch**. If we select that option, when we double-click on the executable to run it, it will not run and will wait for the debugger to connect. For our example, we will only select **Enable debugging option**.

3. On the EXE machine, double-click on your executable to run it. While it is running, open the LabVIEW development system on the DEV machine. In the startup window, select **Operate | Debug Application or Shared Library**. The **Debug Application or Shared Library** dialog appears, and we enter the IP address of the EXE machine and click on **Refresh**. Under **Application or shared library**, the name of the executable that is running on the EXE machine will appear, click on **Connect**. See the following screenshot for an example:

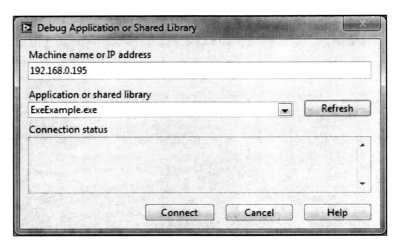

4. After the connection is established, the front panel of the executable will appear on the DEV machine. On the front panel, we right-click and select **Remote Debugging | Show Block Diagram**. See the following screenshot for an example. When the block diagram is shown, we can use all the debugging tools in LabVIEW.

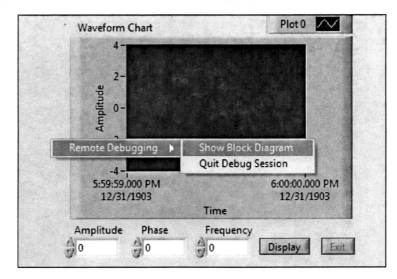

5. If we cannot make the connection, the EXE machine could have a firewall that is preventing the DEV machine from connecting. To resolve this problem, we can open port 3580 through the Windows Firewall for NI Service Locator. If this approach fails, we can install the LabVIEW development software in the EXE machine and connect to the local host (to itself) for debugging.

How it works...

To debug an executable on a machine that does not have the LabVIEW development environment installed, a debug version executable can be deployed and connected to another computer, that is on the same network and with the LabVIEW development environment installed.

Compiling a standalone application

After we compile an executable and deploy it on a machine, we cannot run the executable immediately. We must set up the machine with the correct software before we can run the executable. It is troublesome if we have to install multiple software on the machine before we can run the executable. In this recipe, we will learn how to package the executable with the required software into one installer, so that we only need to double-click on the installer and everything will be installed automatically.

How to do it

A standalone application is just an installer that comprises an executable and drivers required by the executable. We will use an executable that we created previously.

1. We will open the project **ExeExample.lvproj** from the recipe where we learned how to compile an executable. We right-click on **Build Specification** and select **New | Installer**; the **My Installer Properties** dialog, where we can set up the properties of the installer, appears.

2. In the **Product Information** category, we specify the **Build specification** name with ExeExampleInstaller, **Product name** with ExeExample, and **Installer destination** with a convenient place for the example.

3. In the **Destination** category, we can set up where the content of our program will go. We will use the default setting, and that will create a folder inside the **Program Files** folder in your local drive.

4. In the **Source Files** category, we select the executable and all relevant files on the left and transfer them to the right.

How it works...

In a compiled standalone application, it can be sent as an installer to deploy onto another machine. In the installer, everything that is needed to execute a program is included. The user only needs to double-click on the received installer, and the program with all its dependencies will be installed automatically.

In the **Additional Installers** category, we select all the additional installers that our program needs during execution. At the very least, the **NI LabVIEW Run-Time Engine** is needed. If you used other features such as DAQmx, VISA, FPGA, and so on, more installers will be needed. If you are unsure about what is needed, click on each installer and read its description to see whether the installer describes a feature in our code or not.

2
Customizing the User Interface

In this chapter, we will cover:

- ▶ Customizing controls
- ▶ Adding a menu for runtime
- ▶ Creating a dialog
- ▶ Sizing the dialog automatically
- ▶ Using 2D picture control
- ▶ Updating controls with an action engine
- ▶ Creating a simple animation
- ▶ Creating subpanels

Introduction

This chapter presents tips on creating a user interface. We will demonstrate different UI features in UI design, such as customizing a control, adding runtime menu, creating a dialog, using 2D picture control, creating simple animation, and creating subpanels. Ways to manage UI, such as sizing a dialog automatically and updating controls with action engine, will also be demonstrated.

Customizing controls

In LabVIEW, there are different styles of controls to choose from. Control styles such as classic, modern, and so on would fulfill the majority of UI design needs. In addition, there are other styles that can be downloaded from OpenG. Nevertheless, at times, we need a control to look in a particular way and we can customize such special controls in LabVIEW.

Getting ready

To complete this recipe, the LabVIEW development environment is required. In this example, LabVIEW 2012 is used. To customize the numeric control, one picture of a blue car and one picture of a yellow car are needed.

How to do it...

Follow the given steps to implement the recipe:

1. Open a new project and VI.
2. We will start building the front panel. To create a track with a race car, right-click on the front panel and go to **Classic | Numeric | Horizontal Slide**.
3. Right-click on the control and select **Make Type Def**.
4. Right-click on the control and select **Open Type Def**.
5. In the type def, click on **Change to Customize Mode** (wrench icon).
6. Right-click on the knob and select **Import from File at Same Size**, as shown in the following screenshot:

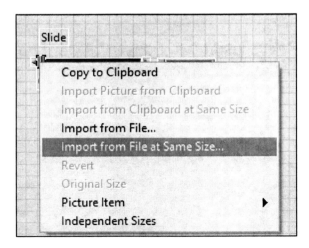

7. Browse to the blue car image and adjust the size of the car.

8. Right-click on the control and select **Change to Indicator**.

9. Save the control and go to **File | Apply Changes**.

10. Repeat steps 2-8 for the yellow car image.

11. To create a signal that starts/stops the race, right-click on the front panel and go to **Modern | Boolean | Round LED**.

12. Right-click on **Round LED** and select **properties**.

13. Keep the On color as green and change Off color to red.

14. Enable **Show boolean text and Multiple strings**.

15. For the On text, type **GO**, and for the Off Text, write **STOP**.

16. Left-click on LED and drag its corner to enlarge it.

17. Right-click on the control and select **Change to Indicator**.

18. To create a status indicator, right-click on the front panel and go to **Classic | String & Path | Simple String**.

19. To make the surrounding of the Simple String transparent, press *Ctrl + Shift +* right-click on the front panel and select the coloring tool.

20. With the coloring tool, right-click on the surrounding of the Simple String indicator and select transparency for both background and foreground color. We get to see the following screenshot for the front panel after executing steps 1-17:

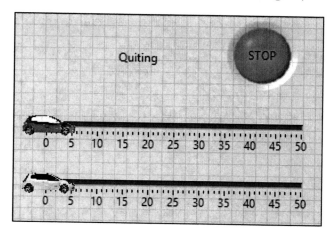

21. The front panel is completed, and we will work on the block diagram. We will use the state machine architecture. We will start by placing a while loop in the block diagram, and place a case structure within the while loop.

22. Create and save a `enum` type def. with states: Initialize, Idle, Run, Done, and Quit.

23. For the while loop, create four shift registers by right-clicking and selecting **Add Shift Register**; one for **BlueCar**, one for **YellowCar**, one for the **Result**, and one for the **State**. Wire these four registers and set the state shift register to **Initialize**. Place a `Wait Until Next ms Multiple` node inside the while loop and wire 500 ms to it. Create a local variable for the **Trigger** Boolean control and set it to `false` to initialize it. The stop condition is set with the Boolean default value, which is a `false`. The state machine and its **Initialize** state are shown in the following screenshot:

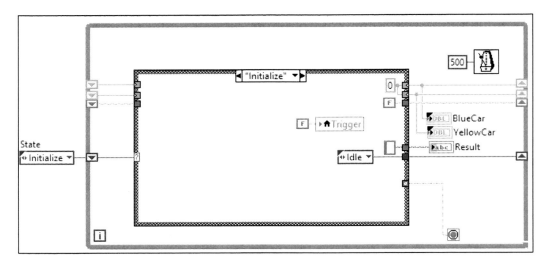

24. Build the **"Idle"** state with an event structure, as shown in the following screenshot:

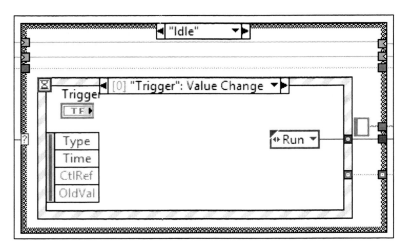

25. Build the second event case within the **Idle** state, as shown in the following screenshot:

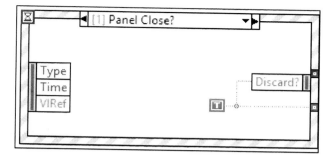

26. Build the **"Run"** state, as shown in the following screenshot:

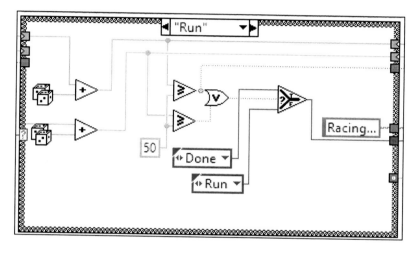

27. Build the **"Done"** state, as shown in the following screenshot:

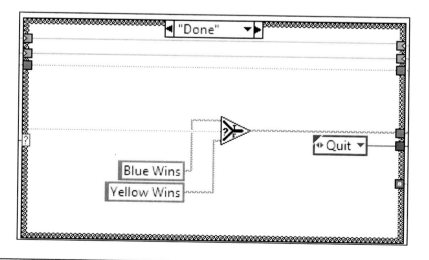

28. Build the **"Quit"** state, as shown in the following screenshot:

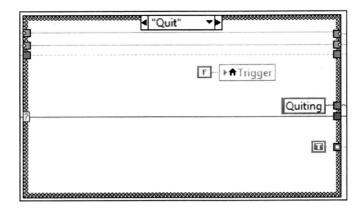

How it works...

The program shown in the previous section is a racing simulation. Two customized controls with yellow and blue race cars are created, and they are driven by random numbers. A big LED is used to start the race, and the status of the race is shown with a simple string indicator. The images of the race cars were obtained from the Internet and a free software called GIMP (http://www.gimp.org/) was used to make the background of the images transparent. For the status indicator, a Classic Simple String is used so that the background can be colored as transparent; the background will not show up and surround the car. To work with images in LabVIEW, Portable Network Graphics (png) format is preferred.

The program starts with the **Initialize** state to initialize all indicators and shift registers, and it proceeds to the **Idle** state. In the **Idle** state, it has an event structure. The program will not pass this state unless **Trigger** has a value change event. Once the Trigger value is changed, the program moves to the **Run** state. If the **Panel Close?** filter event occurs instead, the program will discard the **Panel Close?** event and stop the program. In this case, the **Panel Close?** event is filtered out, so the panel will not close. In the **Run** state, two separate random number generators are used to accumulate the distance traveled by each car. If either of cars crosses the finish line (within 50 ms), the program moves to the **Done** state; if not, the program comes back to the **Run** state. If the blue car wins, a Boolean value true is the output. If the yellow car wins, a Boolean value false is the output. The **Done** state will output the result based on the Boolean value and transit the program into the **Quit** state, where the program wraps everything up.

See also

▶ For more information on the state machine architecture, refer to *Chapter 3, Working with Common Architectures*

Adding a menu for runtime

To make a program more professional, runtime menu is essential. In this recipe, we will create a program with runtime shortcut menu that is invoked by right-clicking on an indicator, and a runtime menu that resides on the top menu bar of the program.

How to do it...

Follow the given steps to create the example for this recipe:

1. Open a new project and VI.

2. Create a chart indicator by right-clicking on the front panel and navigate to **Modern | Graph | Waveform Chart**.

3. Create a Boolean stop by right-clicking on the front panel and navigating to **Modern | Boolean | Stop Button**. First, we will start by creating a right-click shortcut menu for the chart.

4. Right-click on the chart and go to **Advanced | Run-Time Shortcut Menu | Edit...**.

5. In the editor, select **Custom** in the top menu bar.

6. Under **Item Properties**, select **User** under **Item Type** and enter Increment as the **Item Name**.

7. Click on the add button on the top left to add another menu entry.

8. Under **Item Properties**, select **User** under **Item Type** and enter Decrement as the **Item Name**.

9. Click on the add button on the top left to add another menu entry.

10. Under **Item Properties**, select **Separator** under **Item Type**.

11. Click on the add button on the top left to add another menu entry.

12. Under **Item Properties**, go to **Application item | Visible Items | Entire Menu**.

13. Navigate to **File | Save | Save to file** and save the menu as `RunTimeShortcut.`
    `rtm` in the same folder as the VI. The following screenshot is of a completed
    Shortcut Menu:

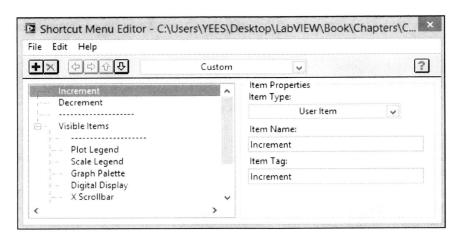

14. After we finish the right-click shortcut menu, we will proceed to adding a custom
    top menu bar.

15. To create custom top menu bar for the front panel, go to **Edit | Run-Time Menu...**.

16. In the editor, select **Custom** in the top menu bar.

17. Under **Item Properties**, select **User** under **Item Type** and enter `Tasks` as the
    Item Name.

18. Click on the add button on the top left to add another menu entry.

19. Under **Item Properties**, select **User** under **Item Type** and enter `Multiplied`
    `by 2` as the **Item Name**.

20. Click the right arrow to make `Multiplied by 2` a subitem of `Tasks`.

21. Click on the add button on the top left to add another menu entry.

22. Under **Item Properties**, select **User** under **Item Type** and enter `Divided by 2`
    as the **Item Name**.

23. Click on the right arrow to make `Multiplied by 2` a subitem of `Tasks`.

24. Go to **File | Save** and save the file as `RunTimeTop.rtm` in the same folder as the VI.

25. Create the front panel as shown in the following screenshot:

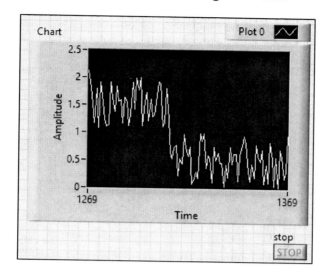

26. Create the block diagram as shown in the following screenshot:

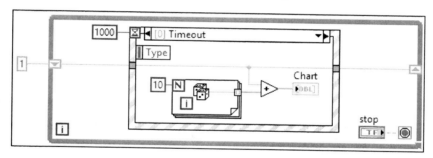

27. Create the second event case, **"Chart": Shortcut Menu Selection (User)**, as shown in the following screenshot. For the inner case structure, the **"Decrement"** case is shown. The case structure has two more cases that are not shown: Increment and Default. For the Increment case, use the increment node. For the Default case, just wire the input wire through.

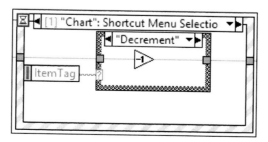

28. Create the last event case as shown in the following screenshot. For the inner case structure, the **"Divided by 2"** case is shown. The case structure has two more cases that are not shown. They are Multiplied by 2 and Default. For the Multiplied by 2 case, use the multiply node with 2 and the input wire as inputs. For the Default case, just wire the input wire through.

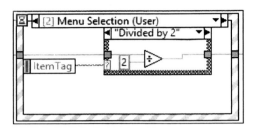

How it works...

The program generates random numbers and displays them on a chart. The user can choose to scale or shift the numbers on the chart.

The event structure has three cases. The timeout case is triggered once every second, and it will generate an array of 10 random numbers and displays them on a chart. If the user right-clicks on the chart and selects **Increment/Decrement**, the shortcut menu selection event is triggered, and the values of the chart are shifted accordingly. If the user selects the **Tasks** menu at the top and selects **Multiplied/Divided by 2**, the menu selection event is triggered and the values of the chart are scaled accordingly.

Creating a dialog

Dialog is a simple pop up that will gather information from user for the program. In this recipe, we will create a simple dialog.

How to do it...

Dialog is a SubVI that would pop up to gather information. To create a simple dialog, we need to execute the following steps:

1. Create a new project and VI.

2. Create the front panel as shown in the next screenshot. The set of controls on the right are within a type-def. cluster and it needs to be created and saved.

3. To set the default values for all the controls, we can either write a value to each control by using a local variable, or set a default value manually. To set a default value manually, enter the default value into the control. Right-click on the control. Select **Data Operations** and **Make Current Value to Default**.

4. On the front panel, click on the upper-right corner of the 4 x 2 x 2 x 4 connector pane and then click on Info Cluster to position the **Info Cluster** on the connector pane.

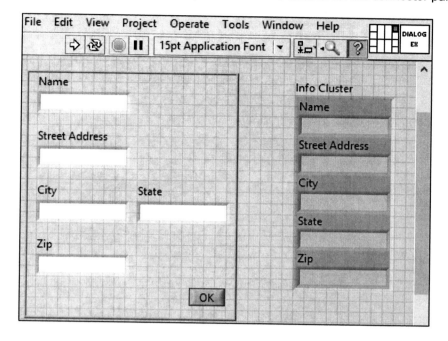

5. Create the block diagram as shown in the following screenshot:

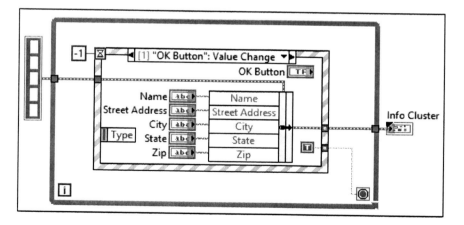

6. On the front panel top menu bar, go to **File | VI Properties**. In the edit dialog, select the **Dialog** option. Check the following screenshot. Under **Window Run-Time Position**, we can select at what location of the monitor the dialog appears.

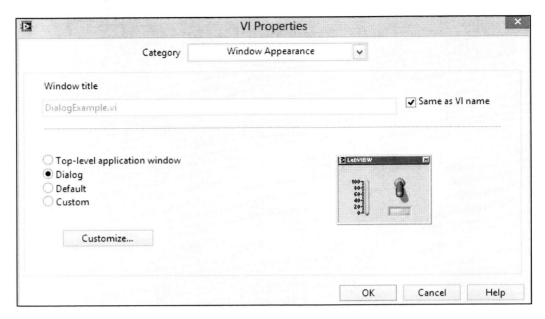

7. Resize the front panel so that the cluster is out of sight.

8. To use the dialog VI in other applications, we simply drop the dialog VI into the application and wire up all the inputs and outputs. When the application execution flow arrives at the dialog VI, it will pop up and gather the information intended.

How it works...

This VI is used as a SubVI inside a program. When the program calls this dialog VI, the dialog pops up, and the program thread that depends on the data of the dialog stops. The user would enter all the information and click on **OK**. The program populates a cluster and passes the data out of SubVI and into the program that calls it.

To make the dialog pop up, its appearance must be set to dialog inside VI properties. The option causes the VI to show it in the front panel during execution. Creating controls to get data from users and use a cluster to pass this data seems redundant. It is possible to use a cluster to get and pass the user data. However, when the controls are within the cluster, it has less flexibility for decoration.

See also

▸ If dialog is used to display a message without needing to gather information from users while allowing the program to continue, a dynamically-called dialog should be used. For further reference on this topic, refer to the *Calling a VI dynamically* recipe in *Chapter 3, Working with Common Architectures*

Sizing the dialog automatically

The size of the dialog is adjusted and saved manually, so that only what is intended to be seen is shown when the dialog appears. However, every time when a dialog is modified, the size may need to be adjusted again. To avoid the trouble of adjusting the front panel every time when a change is made, this recipe provides a way to size a dialog automatically.

How to do it...

To start building the VI to size a dialog automatically, we need to execute the following steps:

1. We open a new project and VI.

2. Create the block diagram as shown in the following screenshots. The six values contained in enum are Initialize, Find Max Height, Set Origin, Set Panel Bounds, Center FP, and Shutdown. The first state **Initialize** gets the VI reference for the front panel which we would like to autosize. The pane reference is obtained, assuming that there is only one pane on the front panel. The references for all the decorations on the front panels are obtained.

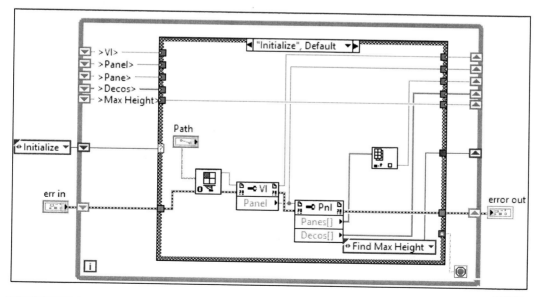

3. Create the next case, **"Find Max Height"**. It examines the height of all the decoration on the front panel and extracts the reference of the decoration with the maximum height. Refer to the following screenshot:

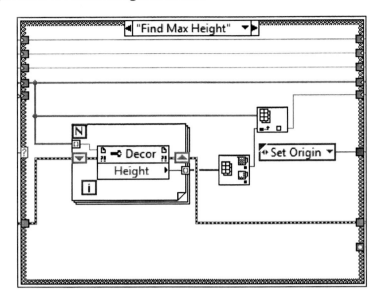

4. Create the next case **"Set Origin"**, as shown in the following screenshot. It sets the origin of the front panel pane to the upper-left hand corner of the largest decoration:

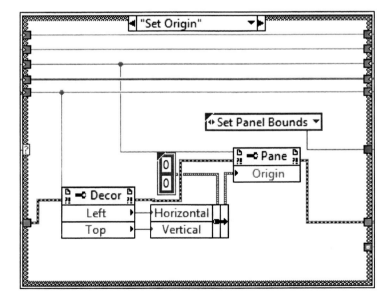

5. Create the next case **"Set Panel Bounds"**, as shown in the following screenshot. It sets the front panel bound to the largest decoration.

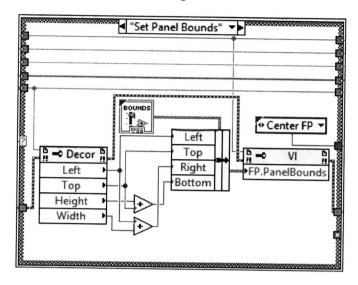

6. Create the next case **"Center FP"**, as shown in the following screenshot. It centers the front panel when shown on the monitor.

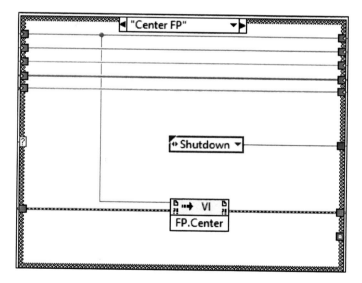

7. Create the final state **"Shutdown"**, as shown in the following screenshot. It closes all the references from property nodes used in previous states. It stops the state machine by setting the stop condition to true.

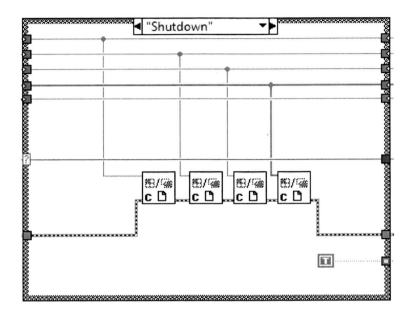

8. In the front panel, connect the path control used in the **Initialize** state to the upper-left hand corner of the terminals pattern. See the following screenshot:

9. Let's build a VI that uses the SubVI we built in steps 1-8. Build the front panel as shown in the following screenshot:

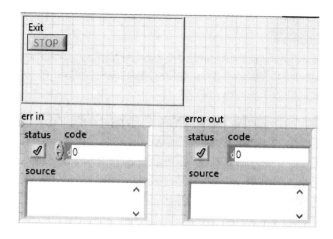

10. Build the block diagram as shown in the following screenshot:

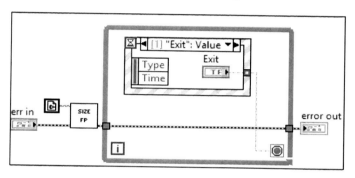

How it works...

This recipe builds a SubVI `AutoResizeVI.vi` that is called by another VI to resize its front panel around a decoration frame. It uses a simple state machine as its architecture.

First, the state machine enters the **Initialize** state to open the references of the caller VI, caller VI's panel, caller VI's Pane, and caller VI's decorations on its front panel. The next **Find Max Height** state, the reference for the decoration with the max height is extracted from the decoration references array. In the next state **Set Origin**, the coordinates of the upper-left hand corner of the decoration is set to be the Pane's origin. In the next state **Set Panel Bounds**, the boundary of the decoration is set equal to the boundary of the front panel. In the **Center FP** state, the front panel is moved to the center of the monitor. Finally, in the **Shutdown** state, all references are closed, and the stop condition for the while loop is set to `true` to exit the program.

In the caller VI, it calls `AutoSize.vi` to resize its front panel to the size of its decoration. Then, it will wait for the user to click on **exit** to leave the program.

▶ This recipe uses the state machine. For more information on the state machine architecture, refer to the *Using the state machine architecture* recipe in *Chapter 3, Working with Common Architectures*

Using 2D picture control

In some test applications, it is beneficial to display test data in a real-time map, which contains test results with location information. For example, if we were to test a batch of products arranged in a rectangular grid, using a map to display data will provide a very good visual to display the location of the product and its test result. In this recipe, we will create a map that shows the test results for products in different coordinates, with the results shown in different colors.

How to do it...

In this example, we will create a VI that calculates all the coordinates where we would like to map our test results. First, we will create a VI to calculate the coordinates.

1. Create the Coordinates.vi VI to generate an array of coordinates used for Draw Rectangle.vi. See the following screenshot:

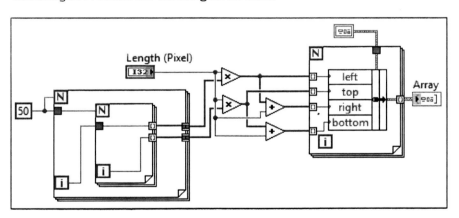

2. Create the main VI that calls Coordinates.vi. See the following screenshot:

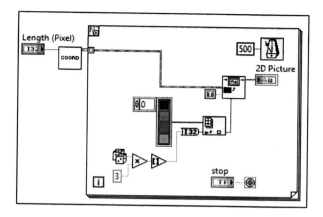

3. Right-click on 2D picture control and deselect **Erase First**.

How it works...

The example creates a 1D array of information to draw 50 x 50 rectangles in a large rectangular drawing area with `Coordinates.vi`. In each element of the array, it contains the top, bottom, left, and right of the rectangle in pixel.

The 1D array is indexed by a for loop that randomly draws each rectangle in the array with a different color. The 2D picture indicator is set to not erase every time it draws, so all rectangles will show up in the 2D picture indicator. See the following screenshot for a map drawn with rectangles with 8 pixels on each side:

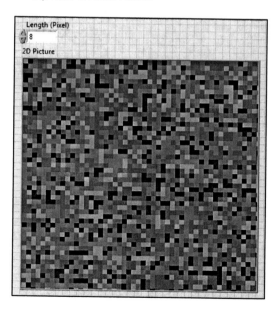

Updating controls with an action engine

A complex application could consist of SubVIs that are multiple layers deep. It would be difficult for such a SubVI to update an indicator of the main VI. In this recipe, we will demonstrate an example to update controls of a main VI from a SubVI through an action engine.

How to do it...

Let's create the action engine. We will start with the **Initialize** command.

1. Create the action engine as shown in the following screenshot. The first command is **Initialize**. It obtains the reference of the VI with controls which we would like to update, obtains its panel reference, and the references of all the controls on the front panel of the VI.

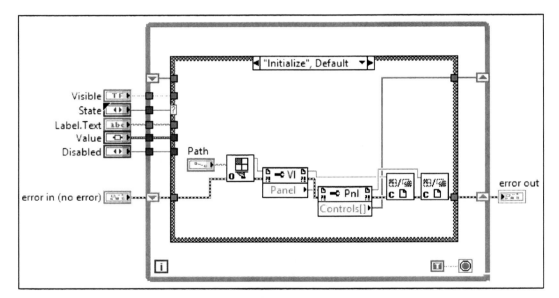

2. Create the next command **"Update Value"** of the action engine, as shown in the following screenshot. With the label of a control, it finds the reference associated with the control, and update the value of the control. This is done on the control that the user would like to update.

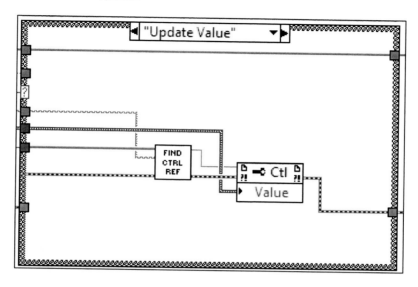

3. Create `FindControlRef.vi` that is used in the preceding action case. It is used in other action cases as well. It extracts the control reference of the user-specified control. The build-in VI, called "Open VI Object Reference", can also perform the same function. See the following screenshot:

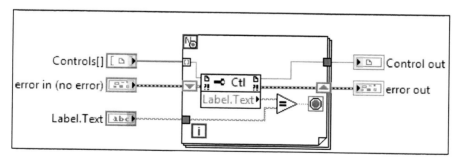

4. Create the next action case **"Update DisEnable"**, as shown in the following screenshot. It finds the reference of the control with label that the user specified and then enables/disables the control as specified by the user.

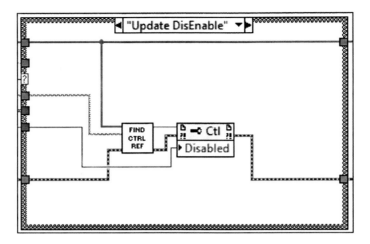

5. Create the next action case **"Update InVisible"**, as shown in the following screenshot. It finds the reference of the control with label that the user specified and then makes the control invisible/visible as specified by the user.

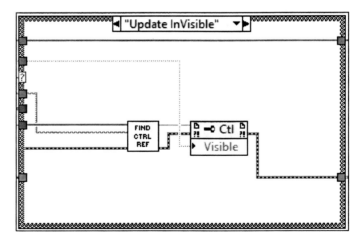

6. Create the last action case **"Shutdown"**, as shown in the following screenshot. It closes all the references of the controls on the front panel.

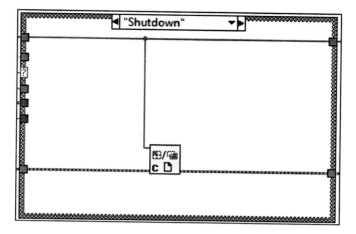

7. Create the example, as shown in the following screenshot, to use the action engine:

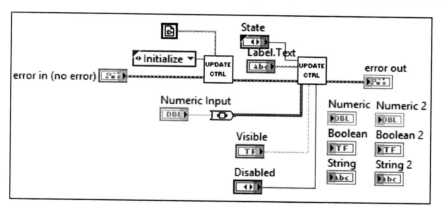

How it works...

The action engine performs three functions: update value, visible status, and enable status of controls. It has two other functions as well: **Initialize** and **Shutdown** for configuration purposes. To use the action engine, the **Initialize** function needs to be executed first, so that all the references of the front panel controls are saved in the action engine. When the action engine is no longer needed, the **Shutdown** function is executed to close all the references. The other functions allow users to update the value, visible state, and enable state of a control by referring to its name. The example shows how the action engine is used.

See also

▸ To learn more about action engine, refer to the *Creating an action engine* recipe in *Chapter 3, Working with Common Architectures*

Creating a simple animation

A picture is worth a thousand words, and an animation is worth even more. In this recipe, we will create a simple animation with a picture ring.

Getting ready

To complete this recipe, the LabVIEW development environment is required. In this example, LabVIEW 2012 is used. For the animation, a set of fan blades pictures that are differed by 30 degrees are needed from 0 to 330 degree (12 pictures total). The pictures must be sized appropriately for the application.

How to do it...

We will start by creating the picture ring with snapshots of a blade's motion, which we will iterate through to create the animation:

1. Create a picture ring by right-clicking on the front panel and navigating to **Classic | Ring & Enum | Pict Ring**.
2. Drag the fan blade picture at 0 degree into the picture ring.
3. Right-click on the picture ring and select **Add Item**.
4. Repeat steps 2 and 3 until all pictures are added. For the last picture, step 3 is to be omitted.
5. Right-click on the control and select **Make Type Def**. Open the type def. and save it in the application folder.
6. Create the example, as shown in the following screenshot, to use the picture ring:

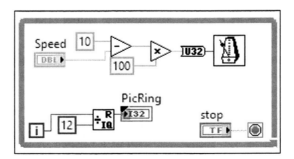

7. The front panel of the example is shown in the following screenshot. Use the decoration to create the base of the fan:

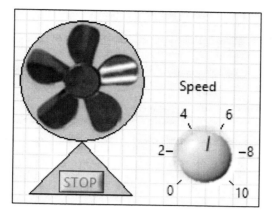

How it works...

The animation is created by looping through and displaying a series of pictures in a loop. The example allows users to change the speed of the fan and to stop the fan with the stop Boolean.

Creating subpanels

Using subpanels allows the flexibility to embed multiple VIs into one at runtime. In this recipe, we will demonstrate how to use subpanels.

How to do it...

We need to perform the following steps to make use of subpanels:

1. Create the state machine, as shown in the following screenshot. The first state **Initialize** creates three VI references by opening the VI template `SimpleAnimationExample.vit` three times. Only a VI template can be opened in this manner to create three VI references.

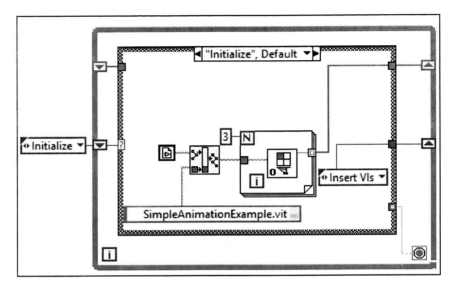

2. Create the next state **"Insert VIs"**, as shown in the following screenshot. It builds an array with the references of the three subpanels that are on the front panels. The for loop inserts the three VIs opened previously into the subpanels.

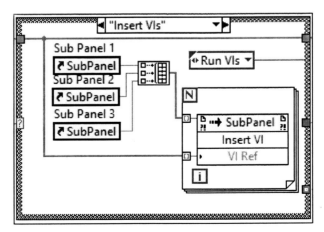

3. Create the next state **"Run VIs"**, as shown in the following screenshot. It runs the VIs inserted into the subpanels.

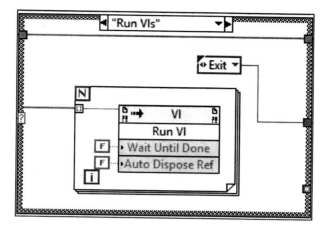

4. Create the next state **"Exit"**, as shown in the following screenshot. It contains an event structure that will wait for the user to exit the program indefinitely.

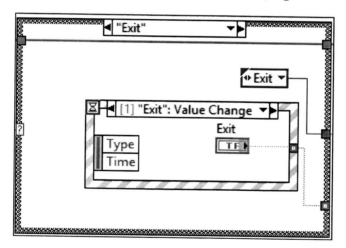

▶ In the previous recipe, open **SimpleAnimationExample.vi** and do a save as `*.vit` in another file. This recipe will call this template into the memory three times for three subpanels, and each time a new reference is generated. See the following front panel of the example:

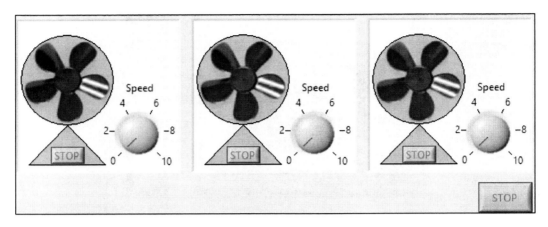

How it works...

This example loads three separate instances of **SimpleAnimationExample.vi** into memory so that they can be executed independently. The example uses the state machine. It enters into the **Initialize** state first, and uses the template file **SimpleAnimationExample.vit** created previously to create three instances of the same VI. The next state, **Insert Vis**, inserts all the subpanels references into an array and iterates through each element in the array to insert the VIs into the subpanels. The next state, **Run Vis**, starts the VIs in each subpanel. **Wait Until Done** is set to `false`, so the program will not wait for the reference VI to finish running before proceeding. **Auto Dispose Ref** is set to `false`, so the main program that calls the reference VI is responsible to dispose of the references of referenced VIs. The last state, **Exit**, waits for the user to click on exit to terminate the program.

See also

▶ This recipe uses a state machine and dynamically calls VI. For more information on the state machine, refer to the *Using the state machine architecture and Calling a VI dynamically* recipe in *Chapter 3, Working with Common Architectures*

3
Working with Common Architectures

In this chapter, we will cover:

- ▸ Working with a case structure
- ▸ Working with an event structure
- ▸ Working with loops
- ▸ Using the state machine architecture
- ▸ Using the master slave architecture
- ▸ Using the producer consumer architecture
- ▸ Creating a SubVI
- ▸ Creating an action engine
- ▸ Calling a VI by reference
- ▸ Calling a VI dynamically
- ▸ Creating a reentrant VI

Introduction

This chapter presents commonly-used architectures and tools. Basic building blocks such as case structure, event structure, loops, SubVI, action engine, dynamically called VI, and reentrant VI are covered in detail to ensure that we are proficient in using these building blocks in LabVIEW. Common architectures such as state machine, master slave, and producer consumer are covered to ensure that we can structure our code in a readable and efficient fashion.

Working with a case structure

Case structure is equivalent to a conditional statement in a text-based programming language. We will create a few case structures that take different kinds of inputs, such as Boolean, numeric, string, enum, and error, to present different features of a case structure.

How to do it...

We will start with a Boolean case structure.

1. The case structure in the following block diagram shows a case structure taking a Boolean input. It consists of **False** and **True** cases. The select node is also in the diagram to show that it can be used instead of a case structure when the input is Boolean. The select node will choose which input to output based on the Boolean input, similar to the case structure.

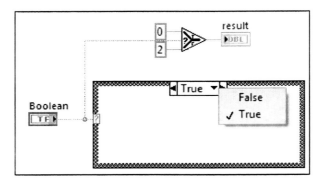

2. The case structure in the following block diagram takes an integer as input. Keep in mind that when the input is a floating point value, it is converted into an integer. The **..-1** case will be executed when the input is less than or equal to 1. The **1, 2** case will be executed when the input is 1 or 2. The **3..5** case will be executed when the input value is between 3 and 5 inclusively. The **6..** case will be executed when the input is greater than or equal to 6. The **0, Default** case will be executed when the input is 0 or does not meet the conditions of all the other cases, which is what **Default** means in this case.

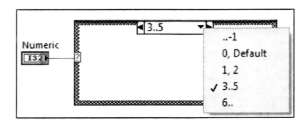

3. The following block diagram shows a case structure with a string input. The **"a".."f"** case will be executed when the ASCII hex value of the input string is between a and f, including a, but excluding f. The **"f".."j"** case will be executed when the ASCII hex value of the input string is between f and j, including f, but excluding j. If the input value does not meet the conditions of the previous states, the **Default** case will run.

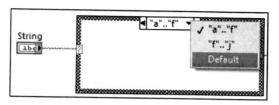

4. The following block diagram shows a case structure with enum input. These cases will be executed based on the input value. The **Case 1** case is assigned as the default case. If the input does not meet the condition of **Case 2** and **Case 3**, Case 1 will run by default. Enum is used for state machine, as it allows for self-documenting code. The value of an enum is also part of its type, so if we add a value in an enum type-def, the change will propagate to the rest of the block diagram.

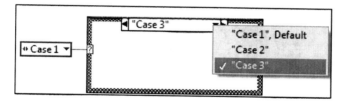

5. The following block diagram contains an error cluster input. It has two cases: **No Error** and **Error**. It is used extensively in a SubVI for bypassing input error, so that it doesn't get corrupted inside the SubVI.

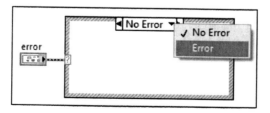

How it works...

Case structure is the main way to make decisions in LabVIEW's code. It can take different types of input, such as Boolean, numeric, string, enum, and error cluster. For the Boolean case structure, sometimes it is more convenient to use the select node. It is important to note that the case structure should not be nested with too many layers and each case should be documented. To reduce layers of a case structure, refer to the *Simplifying logic selection* recipe in *Chapter 9, Simplifying Code*.

Working with an event structure

Event structure consists of one or more cases. Codes that are contained within a case are executed when a control event (mouse click, key stroke, and so on) or a user event (software-based event) occurs.

How to do it...

We will create an example that demonstrates using control event and user event for the event structure.

1. The following example contains a numeric control (**Input Num**). When a number is entered, an event is triggered. For the **Input Text** string control, if a string is entered, an event is triggered, but no text will show up, as all the events (entering text) are discarded. When the **Switch** Boolean control is clicked, an event is triggered. If any event is triggered, the string indicator (**Action**) will update with a string that states what event has occurred. The following screenshot shows the front panel of the controls and indicator:

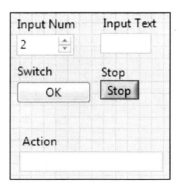

2. The following screenshot shows the block diagram of the example. On the left, a **Create User Event** node is used to create a user event that can be generated within the code. The input user event data type is the data type used for data passing for a user event. We will discuss the data passing aspect of an event structure in the *Using an event structure to pass data* recipe of *Chapter 5, Passing Data*. The label of the data type in our example is **Stop User**, which will be used as the name of the user event. The while loop at the bottom iterates once every **500** ms, and it will generate a user event if the stop Boolean control is set to `true`. The event reference is registered with the `Register for Events` node and fed into the dynamic event terminal, which needs to be enabled by right-clicking on the frame of the event structure and then select **Show Dynamic Event Terminals**. In the top while loop, we see the event case that handles the event when the value of the Boolean changes for the **Switch** control. It is a good practice to put the control associated with the event case into the case, so that the control is easy to find and it is read by the program every time the event is triggered. When the Boolean value changes, the **Action** string indicator will update to show what event has occurred.

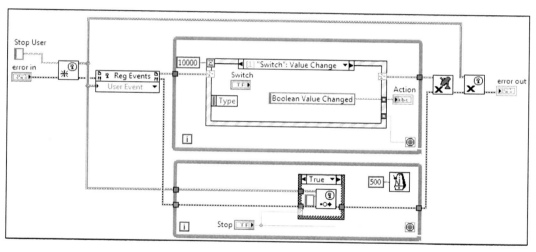

3. The event case in the following screenshot will be executed when a key is pressed within the **Input Num** numeric control. The **Action** string indicator will update and show that the event has occurred.

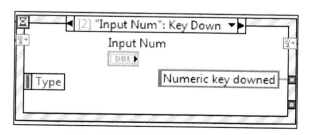

4. To create the previous event case, right-click on the event structure and select **Add Event Case...**. The following screenshot shows how to set up the case. Select the **Input Num** numeric control under **Event Source** and then choose which type of event to handle.

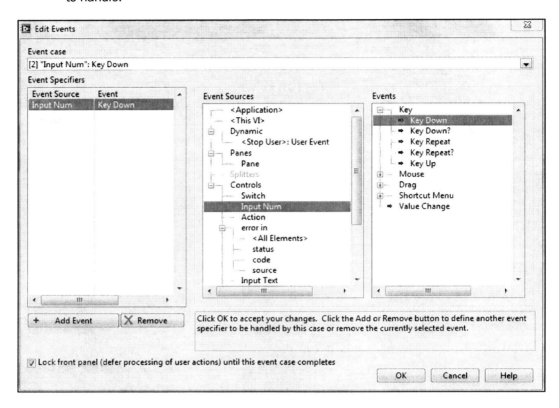

5. The event case in the following screenshot will execute when a key is pressed within the string control, similar to the event case for the numeric control. However, notice **?** behind the label of the **Key Down** event. This is a filter event which can discard the outcome of the event, contrary to all the previous event cases which use notify event. While our example runs as we enter values into the string control, we see that the key down event happened at the string control in the **Action** string indicator. The entered values do not appear in the string controls as the events are discarded.

Filter events give us the ability to trigger based on an event while discarding the event as though it never happened. Notify events will trigger based on an event without interfering with the occurrence of the event.

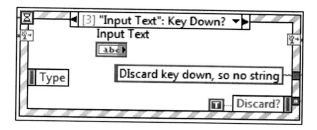

6. The event case in the following screenshot will execute when a timeout event occurs. In this example, the timeout event will occur in 10000 ms, if no other events occur. We can change the timeout value as we wish. If we do not want the timeout event to trigger, we can wire a **-1** to the timeout input.

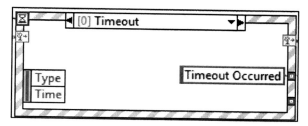

7. The event case in the following screenshot will execute when a user event is generated at the bottom while loop (refer to screenshot of the complete example). Recall that the name of the user event is the label of the data type when we created the user event. The user event is generated by the bottom loop when the stop Boolean control is set to true. This way both loops can stop each other's execution.

8. If we have to create thirty event cases manually, it can be a lot of work. The following screenshot shows an example with thirty Boolean controls. For the example, we don't have to create thirty event cases for each Boolean control. The example gets all the references of the controls on the front panel as an array and registers all the references as a dynamic event. In this event case, if any of the Boolean controls has a value change event, the case will trigger. To get more resolution, we get the reference of the control for which the event originated from and print out a text.

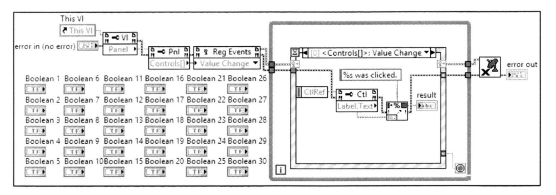

How it works...

Whenever we find ourselves wanting to use a while loop to poll user for data, we should use the event structure instead. When the event structure is waiting for an event, it does not consume any CPU resources.

See also

▶ There is more to event structure. Please proceed to the *Using an event structure to pass data* recipe in *Chapter 5, Passing Data* to see how to use the event structure to pass values.

Working with loops

Loop is a common element in programming. In LabVIEW, there is for loop, while loop, and timed loop with features that facilitate LabVIEW programming. We will go over the for loop. For the while loop, its features are very similar to the for loop, so it is omitted.

How to do it...

The for loop is used when a predetermined number of iteration is needed. For an undetermined number of iteration, use the while loop instead.

1. In the following screenshot, on the left, all the features of a for loop are shown; on the right is shown the result of the example. The input of the for loop is an array with elements 3 and 6. The entry point where the array enters the for loop is a [] symbol, which means autoindexing. When the array is autoindexed, each iteration of the for loop will get an element of the array in order. Since the loop is autoindexed, the **N** symbol (number of iteration) at the upper-left hand corner does not need to be wired. The loop will iterate through each element of the array. In our case, the for loop will iterate two times. If multiple arrays with different lengths are wired into the for loop through autoindex, the number of times that the for loop will iterate is the size of the array with the least number of elements. The **i** would output the current iteration of the loop, and the stop symbol allows the program to stop the loop before completion. For enabling the conditional stop, right-click on for loop and enable the **Conditional** terminal.

2. The example shows four output options. To select an option, right-click on the output terminal, select **Tunnel Mode**, and then select the desired option. For the last value option, the value at the very end of the array is outputted. For the **Indexing** option, the same number of elements as the input is outputted. For the **Conditional** option, we can create conditions for which elements are built into the output array. For the **Concatenation** option, we can concatenate to the end of a 1D array.

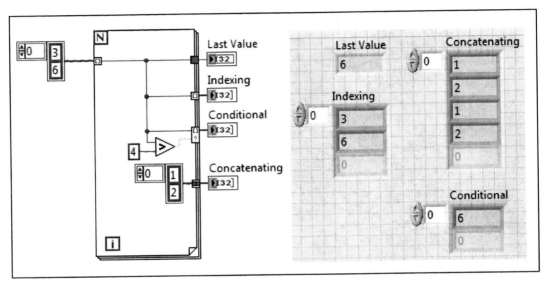

How it works...

The for loop iterates over the same code for a predetermined number of times. If the **Conditional** terminal is enabled, the for loop can be stopped prematurely. The for loop has many features, such as outputting the value of last iteration, indexing through an array (with and without a condition), and concatenating an array, that are useful for array processing.

See also

▸ The for loop has an optimization feature called parallelism. If our code inside the for loop could run in parallel, this feature would help us optimize the code. However, this feature is beyond the scope of this book.

Using the state machine architecture

State machine can transform a piece of sequential code into states with flexible transition between states. In a state machine, the code is self-documented and easy to read. In this recipe, we will use the state machine to program a simple rock-paper-scissors game simulator.

How to do it...

To start a state machine, it is a good idea to draw a flowchart first. Start by executing the following steps:

1. To start, create a flowchart of the example program. See the following screenshot for the flowchart:

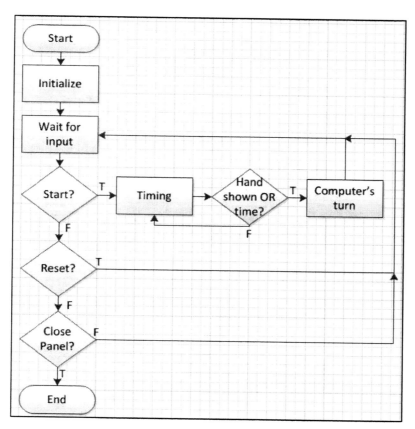

2. Open a new VI and build a state machine, as shown in the following screenshot. Create an enum type-def with values such as **Initialize, Wait for input, Timing, Computer's turn**, and **Shutdown**. To create a type-def, refer to the *Customizing controls* recipe in *Chapter 2, Customizing the User Interface*. In a state machine, an enum is usually used, but a string is used frequently as well. **Wait Until Next ms Multiple** is used to slow down state transition. The state machine starts at the **Initialize** state, which will initialize indicators and shift registers. In this example, we are creating a state machine from scratch, but we can also utilize the state machine template built-in to LabVIEW. To use a template, create a VI by selecting **File and New....**

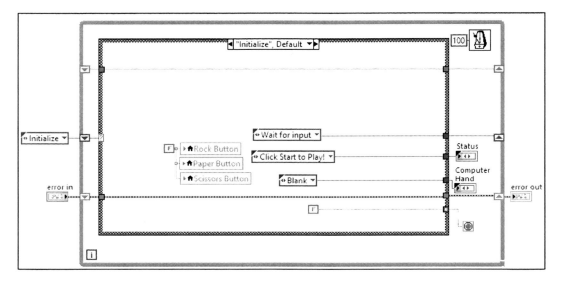

3. The next state is **Wait for input**. It contains an event structure that waits for the user to click on the **Start** button, click on the **Reset** button, or close the panel. When the **Start** button is clicked on, a timer action engine that acts as a timer is started, as shown in the following screenshot:

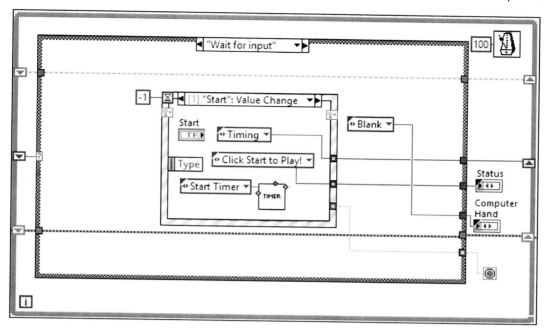

4. When the **Reset** button is clicked, all controls are reset to their default values:

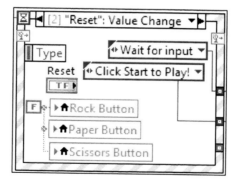

5. When the panel is closed, the action is discarded and the program is stopped, as shown in the following screenshot:

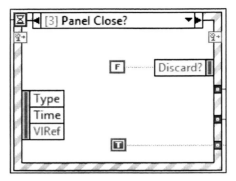

6. The next state is the **"Timing"** state. If a user has decided a hand or when **3** seconds are up, the program transits into the next state. If not, the **Timing** state is revisited:

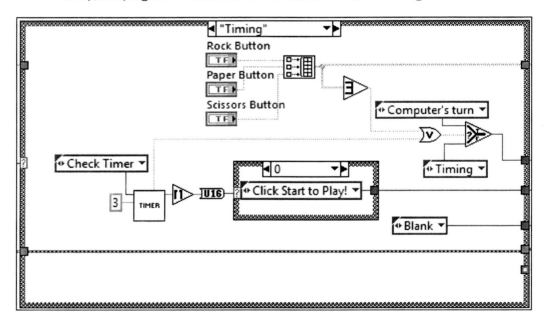

7. The next state **"Computer's turn"** decides the computer's hand and updates the result. If the user selects a hand after three seconds, the computer's hand is determined randomly, as shown in the following screenshot:

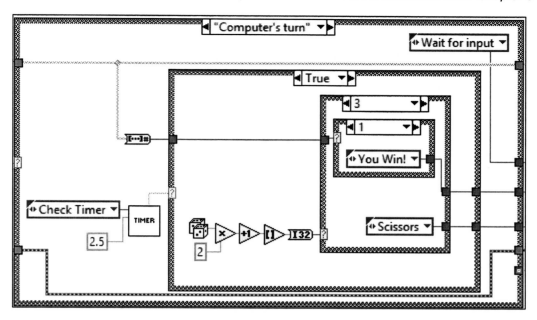

8. However, if the user selects a hand too early, the computer will determine what hand it needs to win the game and select that hand:

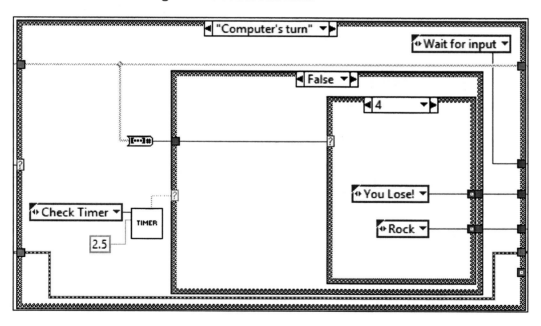

9. Finally, the state machine goes back to the **Wait for input** state.

How it works...

For this program, after the user starts the program, the user would click on **Start** to begin the game. After the **Start** button is clicked on, the user has three seconds to select a hand or lose the game. If the user selects a hand too early, the computer determines the winning hand and selects it. If not, the computer's hand is determined randomly. After a game is completed, the user needs to click on **Reset** before clicking on **Start** for a new game.

In the **Initialize** state, local variables are used to set all controls to their default values. This is one of the few ways that are acceptable to use local variables. In LabVIEW, using local variables to pass data could be dangerous, since a race condition can occur to cause programs to behave erratically. However, to update user interface, local variables do come in handy. In the while loop level, each iteration is slowed down to 100 ms per iteration. If the state machine runs too fast, it can consume too much CPU resources.

In the **Wait for input** state, multiple actions are handled. If the **Start** button is clicked on, a timer is started. This is when the game begins.

After the program transits to the **Timing** state, the program will continue to loop back to it until the user decides a hand or until three seconds are up. The Boolean controls that represent the user's hands are built into an array and converted into a number, so that 1 represents Rock, 2 represents Paper, and 4 represents Scissors, based on binary math.

Next, the program transits into the **Computer's turn** state. The computer will decide a hand and output the result. When a game is done, the program goes back to **Wait for input** for another game.

See also

▶ In this recipe, we used a timer action engine. For more details about the action engine, please refer to the *Creating an action engine* recipe in *Chapter 3, Working with Common Architectures*.

Using the master slave architecture

The master slave architecture consists of at least one master and one slave. The master will notify the slave to perform a task with required information. If multiple slaves are used, the master can notify multiple slaves with the same piece of information simultaneously. In this recipe, we will see an example of how the architecture works.

How to do it...

The master slave architecture used in this example consists of three while loops that employ one notifier for communication amongst themselves.

1. Create the block diagram, as shown in the following screenshot. On the left of the top while loop, the Obtain Notifier node is used to create a notifier and the reference is passed to the loops. The top while loop (master) has an event structure with the Send Notification node in the speak event case. In the other event case, it contains the stop Boolean to terminate the loop. The bottom two while loops (slaves) both output a string from the master, but the first slave would do it 1 second slower. In this example, we are creating a master slave architecture from scratch, but we can also utilize the master slave template built-in to LabVIEW. To use a template, create a VI by selecting **File and New....**

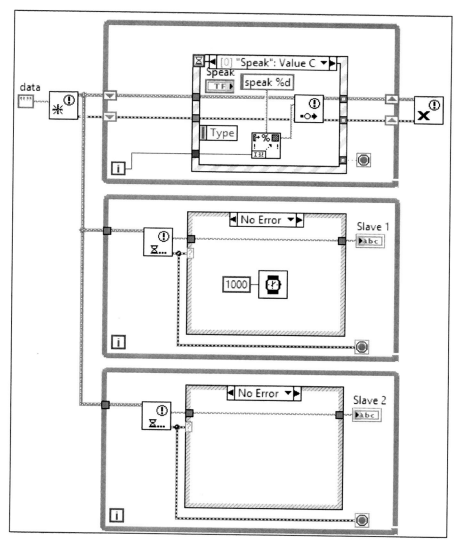

2. The front panel should look like the following screenshot:

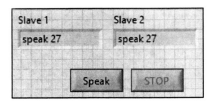

How it works...

This recipe demonstrates how a master/slave architecture works. The master handles the user interface (UI) events. When the **STOP** Boolean is clicked on, the master loop stop condition is met. After the master loop stops, the thread continues and releases the notifier. When the notifier is released, it is no longer valid, so the slave loops that are waiting for notification will send an error to stop the loops.

When the **Speak** button is clicked on, the master sends a message to both slaves. The first slave will display the message in one second, and the second slave will display the message immediately. Before the master sends a notification, the slaves are idle at the Wait on Notification node.

If the user clicks speak once every few seconds, the display is updated as discussed. Even if the user clicks on speak twice without a delay, the displays would still update accordingly, since the ignore previous flags are set to false by default. The Wait on Notification node can still receive a notification that happens before the waiting starts. For example, after slave 1 receives the first notification, it will go into the case structure to output the received string and wait for one second. If during the wait time, another notification occurs, when slave 1 is back to Wait on Notification, the miss event would trigger the slave to output the string and wait for one second again. If the user clicks on **Speak** three times without delay, the second string from the second notification is lost, since it is overwritten by the third notification. Notifications can overwrite each other. If the master sends out more notification than a slave can process in time, some notifications are overwritten. If that's not a big concern, this architecture would be a good choice. If every notification must be addressed by the slaves, a queue-based architecture such as producer and consumer should be considered.

Using the producer consumer architecture

The producer consumer architecture consists of at least one producer and one consumer. The producer would use a queue to pass required information to the consumer and instruct the consumer to start a task. If the consumer cannot attend the instruction, it is queued up and addressed when the consumer is available.

Imagine the consumer as a person sitting at a desk filling out forms, and the producer as a person handing forms to the consumer to fill out. If the consumer is filling out a form and another form is needed to be filled out, the producer will not interrupt the consumer, but simply deliver the new form to the consumer's inbox. The consumer will start working on the form in the inbox once the current form is completed. In contrast, for the master slave architecture, the master can give the same form to two different slaves.

How to do it...

The producer consumer architecture, that is used for the example, consists of two while loops and queue functions to pass data between loops.

1. Build the block diagram as shown in the following screenshot. It creates a queue with string data type. The queue's reference is passed into the producer loop (top) and the consumer loop (bottom). The producer loop contains an event structure, which would enqueue the string element to trigger the consumer to perform a predefined task when the **Enqueue Element** button is clicked on. Notice that the passed string is not used by the consumer. The second event case (not shown) will stop the producer loop when a user clicks on the **Stop** button. The consumer loop would exit when there is an error. An error would occur by design when the user stops the program, the producer loop proceeds to release the queue, and the consumer continues to access the queue. The case structure within the No Error case in the consumer would check how many elements are in the queue and increment a counter to keep track of time.

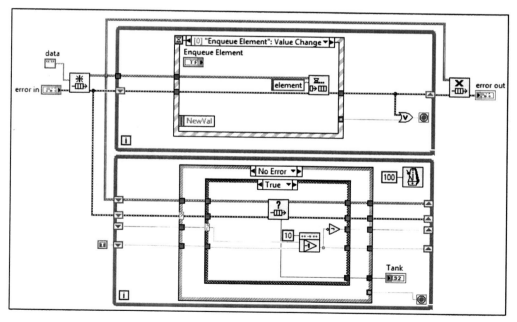

2. The **False** case within the No Error case dequeues an element from the queue and checks how many elements are left in the queue, as shown in the following screenshot:

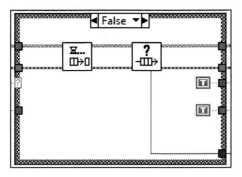

3. The front panel of the program contains a tank indicator that shows how many elements are in the queue and buttons to enqueue and stop the program:

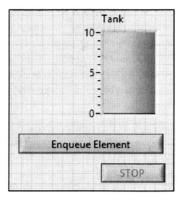

How it works...

This program shows how the producer consumer architecture works. When the user clicks on **Enqueue Element** multiple times, the number of elements in the queue will increase and will be shown in the tank. As the elements in the queue are addressed by the consumer, the level of tank will decrease. One important feature of this architecture is that the elements enqueued are not lost, unless there is an overflow condition. In the consumer, there are four shift registers that pass the data from one iteration to another. The first two are for the queue reference and the error cluster.

The first Boolean decides entering either the true or false case. The **False** case is entered if the counter counts to zero. Since the number of count is 10 and the loop timer is 100 ms, the false case is entered about once every second. The main purpose of the false case is to update the display with the number of elements in queue. The true case would dequeue an element from the queue and update the display.

Creating a SubVI

A complex program should be divided into logical sections into SubVI, so that the program is more manageable and easy to read. SubVI also allows for code reuse, which can save time. In this recipe, we will create a SubVI that zips all files in folder.

How to do it...

We start the SubVI by creating a block diagram, as shown in the following screenshot:

1. Create the block diagram. It creates the ZIP file, adds files into the ZIP file, and closes the ZIP file reference.

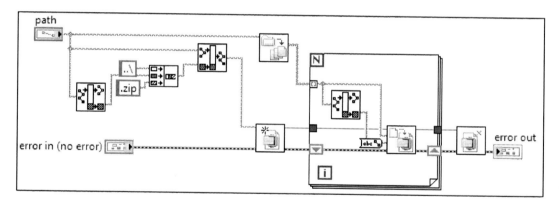

2. Arrange the front panel, as shown in the following screenshot and connect the controls and indicators to the icon terminals:

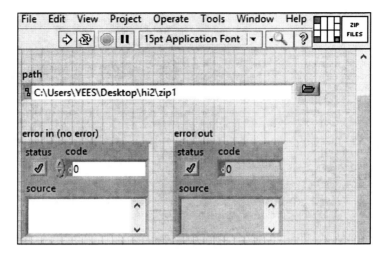

3. Use the icon editor to create the icon, as shown in the following screenshot. The boundary is created by double-clicking on the rectangle tool.

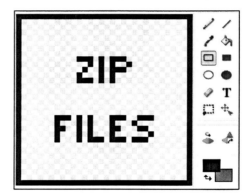

How it works...

When creating the SubVI, it should be loosely coupled and highly cohesive. Loosely coupled means the SubVI is very independent and does not depend on other SubVIs very much. Highly cohesive means all the elements inside the SubVI achieve the same goal.

A terminal pattern should be kept consistent for all your applications. The 4 x 2 x 2 x 4 is highly recommended. The input should be on the left and the output on the right of the icon. At least a simple icon art or text should be placed on the icon, so that its purpose is clear by looking at the icon. Documentation should be placed inside VI properties, so that when a user hovers over the icon with help enabled, documentation can be seen without going into the SubVI.

Creating an action engine

In LabVIEW, using a local or global variable can create a race condition. A race condition is created when a variable is overwritten before it can be read as intended. This happens in LabVIEW, since the execution sequence of a variable cannot be controlled by itself. Functional global variables are preferred for data transfer, which allow a user to set and get data by calling a SubVI. Race condition in an action engine can be eliminated, since its execution sequence can be controlled by wiring its error terminal to enforce data flow. An action engine is a functional global variable with data processing capabilities. Instead of just setting and getting a value, an action engine changes the value as well. In this recipe, we will create a timer action engine.

How to do it...

An action engine is very similar to a state machine, except for the fact that only one state is executed when called in an action engine.

1. Create an **Enum** input, the **Timer Duration** input, and the **Time Elapsed** output. The enum has values such as **Start Timer, Restart Timer, Check Timer,** and **Pause Timer**. The **Start Timer** and **Restart Timer** functions save the current time stamp into a shift register. For **Start Timer**, it will reset **Time Elapsed**. For **Restart Timer, Time Elapsed** is preserved by writing what is in the shift register back into the register. See the following screenshot for details:

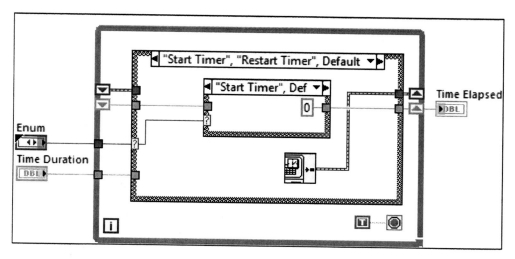

2. The next function is **"Check Timer"**. It determines how much time has lapsed since the **Start Timer** function was called. The **Time Elapsed** function is compared with **Time Duration**. If **Time Elapsed** is greater, the **Time Elapsed** Boolean becomes true, as shown in the following screenshot:

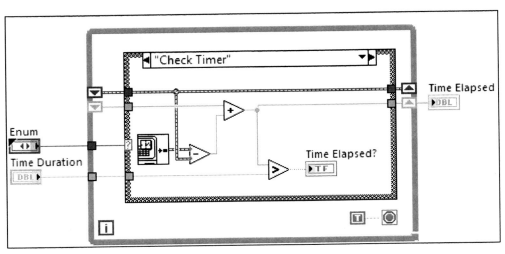

3. The next function **"Pause Timer"** calculates the time difference between **Start Timer** and **Pause Timer** and saves it into a shift register:

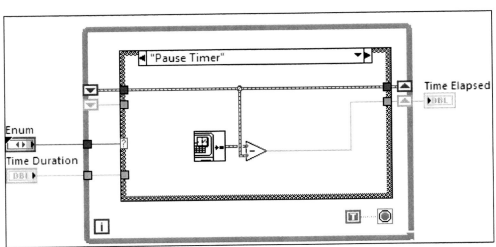

4. To test the action engine, an example is created. It starts the timer, waits for 2.1 seconds, and checks the timer, as shown in the following screenshot:

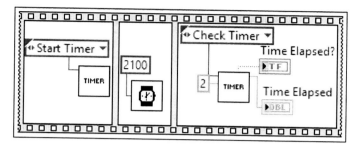

How it works...

Usually, an action engine only performs one action when it is called. Notice that the stop condition of the while loop is set to `true`, so the while loop will only iterate one time and only one case of the case structure is executed. The action engine prevents a racing condition, since it needs to be called in order to set or get its value. Keep in mind that an action engine uses shift register to store values, so its execution mode needs to be set to non-reentrant. If a VI is reentrant, the VI may have multiple copies in the memory. It is possible that a value is set in one copy and read in another, which will produce invalid results.

See also

▸ To see how this timer action engine is used, refer to the *Using the state machine architecture* recipe in *Chapter 3, Working with Common Architectures*. For another example, refer to the *Updating controls with an action engine* recipe in *Chapter 2, Customizing the User Interface*.

Calling a VI by reference

Calling a VI by reference is one way to load a VI into memory as needed. It is also very useful that a VI can be loaded by its filename. In this recipe, we call two different VIs at runtime with the same node.

How to do it...

To start, we will create a VI that will be loaded into memory by reference.

1. Create **NumCapitals.vi** for loading. It counts how many uppercase letters are in the input string.

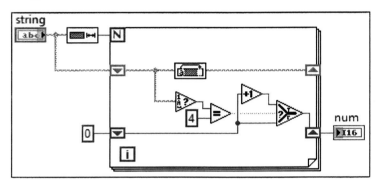

2. Create **Stringlength.vi** with the string length node.
3. Create the main VI that calls **NumCapitals.vi** and **Stringlength.vi** in a loop. The main VI will build the output as an array of cluster, which shows the VI name and its result next to each other.

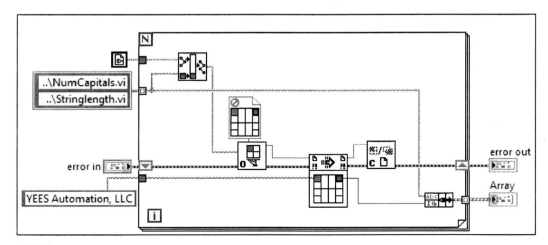

How it works...

By providing a different path to the same call by reference node, two different VIs can be called, given that they have the same terminals arrangement.

The input of the program is **YEES Automation, LLC**. The program calls the **NumCapital.vi** to first count how many upper case letters are in the string. After the path is built, it is used to open a VI reference. The type specifier above the Open VI reference node provides the terminal arrangement information to the VI reference. Having the terminals is like passing values into a SubVI that is dropped directly into the main VI. The VI is loaded when needed and unloaded immediately after its execution is done, so the referenced VI does not reside in the memory for the entire runtime.

Calling a VI dynamically

Dynamically calling a VI is one way to load a VI into memory as needed. In this recipe, we will launch a dialog to display some information. Comparing dynamic loading to loading a VI by reference, it is harder to pass values to a VI that is loaded dynamically, but loading a VI dynamically provides more options in loading.

How to do it...

We will start by creating the VI that will be loaded dynamically.

1. Create a dialog VI with a front panel, as shown in the following screenshot:

2. The dialog VI would execute a while loop for 1 iteration for 3 seconds and close its front panel, as shown in the following screenshot:

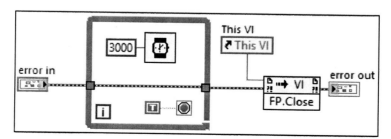

3. To launch the dialog, a launch VI is created. It opens the dialog's VI reference, opens the front panel, and runs it.

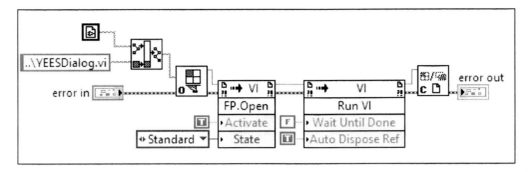

How it works...

When the dialog is launched, it will display for three seconds and close. The dialog has to close its own front panel when it is dynamically called. The dialog is loaded into the memory when needed. It is not loaded when the main program loads, so the memory usage is lowered.

In the launcher VI, it opens the VI reference of the dialog VI. The build-path information shows that the dialog VI is located in the same folder as the launch VI. With the dialog reference, its front panel is opened. Its front panel opens and becomes the active window. The VI starts with the Run VI `Invoke Node`. By setting **Wait Until Done** to false, the launch VI will continue its execution even though the dialog VI is still running. If the main VI is doing some initialization that would take a while, we can launch an advertisement or a process bar to keep the user occupied before the initialization begins, while the main program finishes its initialization. With **Auto Dispose Ref** set to true, the dialog VI takes ownership in disposing itself from memory when done.

See also

▶ For more example, see the *Creating subpanels* recipe in *Chapter 2, Customizing the User Interface*.

Creating a reentrant VI

A reentrant VI is a VI that has a pool of data space shared among multiple instances of the VI. In this recipe, we will create a recursive VI. It is a VI that executes itself. It will calculate the factorial recursively.

How to do it...

To create a VI that will call itself (reentrant VI), we start by creating a case structure with two cases.

1. The first case is shown in the following screenshot:

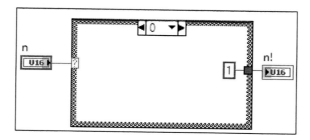

2. Create the second case, as shown in the following screenshot. The SubVI used is self. Its input is **n** and output is **n!**. Connect the input and output to the terminals of the SubVI.

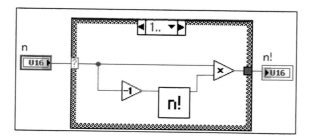

3. Set the Execution setting in VI properties. The Reentrancy setting needs to be set to **Shared clone reentrant execution:**

Category   Execution   ▾

☑ Allow debugging

Reentrancy

○ Non-reentrant execution

◉ Shared clone reentrant execution

○ Preallocated clone reentrant execution

Reentrancy settings affect memory usage, call overhead, jitter, and state maintained within the VI. Display Context help for guidance with selecting the best setting for your use case.

☐ Inline subVI into calling VIs

Priority

normal priority   ▾

Preferred Execution System

same as caller   ▾

☐ Enable automatic error handling

☐ Run when opened

☐ Suspend when called

☐ Clear indicators when called

☐ Auto handle menus at launch

How it works...

For reentrant VIs, there are two settings: **Shared clone reentrant execution** and **Preallocated clone reentrant execution**. For shared clone, if there are 10 instances of the VI, there are 10 or less data spaces, since some of the instances may be sharing data space. When data space is shared, a value saved in a shift register in one instance of the VI may be overwritten by another instance of the VI. This setting is required for recursive VIs. For preallocated clone, if there are 10 instances of the VI, there are 10 data spaces. Each instance of the VI has its own dedicated data space, so data spaces are isolated.

This recipe implements a recursive VI, a type of reentrant to calculate factorial. Since it calls itself, it must contain a case structure with a case that would stop the cycle of calling itself. In our example, the input will get decremented to zero to enter the zero case that doesn't do self call.

A reentrant VI can be used to create recursive VIs. However, it is often used to create VIs that can be called in parallel. If a SubVI is set as non-reentrant, and it is called in two parallel loops, the loops cannot execute in parallel since they are sharing the same SubVI. To cause the parallel loops to execute in parallel, the SubVI needs to become reentrant.

4
Managing Data

In this chapter, we will cover:

- ▶ Using error terminals
- ▶ Using the flat sequence structure
- ▶ Using the feedback node
- ▶ Reusing memory
- ▶ Manipulating an array
- ▶ Using rendezvous
- ▶ Using semaphore

Introduction

This chapter presents tips on managing data. It presents how to create execution sequence with error terminal and how to use flat sequence structure when truly needed. Rendezvous and semaphore are presented for controlling the execution flow of parallel loops. Feedback node and the **In Place Element Structure** reuse memory.

Using error terminals

Error terminals are used to pass error information downstream for further handling. However, they can also be used to enforce sequence in LabVIEW.

How to do it...

To demonstrate how to use error terminals to enforce sequence, we will create a SubVI.

1. Create the SubVI as shown in the following screenshot. It adds two input numbers and outputs the result. The error input connects directly to the error output. The error cluster control/indicator is located in the front panel palette under **Array, Matrix & Cluster**.

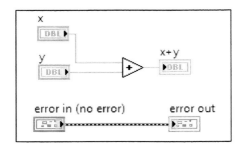

2. Create the example, as shown in the following screenshot, with the SubVI in the previous diagram. The example opens a configuration, puts the result of the SubVI into the **Number** section with **Num1** as the key, and closes the configuration file reference.

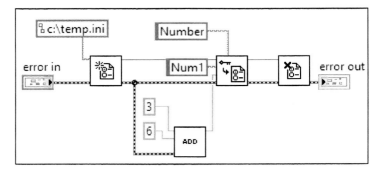

How it works...

The sequence of execution in LabVIEW is different comparing to a text-based language, which executes everything sequentially one line at a time. LabVIEW is data driven. If a piece of code has data, it will run, regardless of where it is on the block diagram. The preceding SubVI shows that an error is fed through the SubVI directly. The SubVI will not execute until it receives error information. Even though the error information is not used directly, it creates a sequence. To see data flow in LabVIEW visually, we can turn on **Highlight Execution** on the block diagram toolbar. Keep in mind that **Highlight Execution** slows down the program, so it affects timing of the program, which can create bugs that only appear during debugging.

In the preceding example, all sections of code wait for data from the left. Starting out with no error as an input, the **temp.ini** file in **c:** is opened. The write ini file node and the add SubVI will execute in parallel, since they both have all the data needed at the same time. Note that if the error input of the add SubVI is not connected to the error output of the open ini file node, the SubVI will execute at the beginning of the program, since it would have all the needed input from the beginning. After the result of the add SubVI is written into the ini file, the file is closed.

Using the flat sequence structure

Flat sequence structure enforces the sequence of a program. Many people use this excessively, which goes against the data flow model of LabVIEW. In this recipe, we will see how to use this structure appropriately.

How to do it...

We will create a small program that measures the execution time of a node:

1. The following screenshot shows a flat sequence structure with three frames. The order of the sequence is from left to right. The first frame on the left uses the "Tick (ms)" node to measure the start time. The second frame contains a "Wait (ms)" node that waits for 1000 ms. The code in this frame is the code that we would like to measure execution time on. The third frame uses the "Tick (ms)" node to measure the time after the "Wait (ms)" node has executed and subtracts the tick from the first frame to calculate the duration of the execution for the second frame.

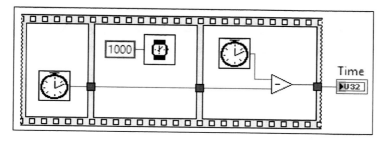

2. Another common way in which a sequence structure is used is shown in the following screenshot. It is a flat sequence structure with only one frame. The error input is wired through the sequence structure directly to the error output. By doing this, a sequence is created with the data flow of the error terminals.

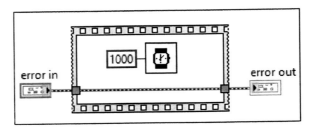

How it works...

The first screenshot shows how the sequence structure is used to determine the execution time of a SubVI. The second frame of the sequence structure has a wait node with 1000 ms. In a real application, a SubVI will take its place, and the execution time of the SubVI will be determined.

In the second screenshot, a single frame sequence structure is used to enclose the wait node. An error cluster is fed through the frame. The code within the single frame will not execute until the error cluster is available. By doing this, execution sequence is enforced by the error terminals. The method is used to enforce sequence when there is a small section of code that does not have data dependency, but it needs to be executed in a particular location of a sequence without using flat sequence structure excessively.

Using the feedback node

The feedback node stores data from one VI execution or loop iteration to the next. It is very similar to a shift register, but has additional features such as different modes of initialization.

How to do it...

We will demonstrate how to use a feedback node by building a simple program that multiplies an input number by the value of a counter.

1. Build the following block diagram. The input **Num to Multiply** is a numeric input, which is multiplied by the value of a counter created by a feedback node to produce **Result**.

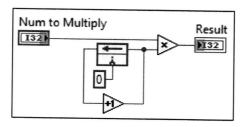

2. The feedback node is initialized to zero. With the feedback node, we can specify when the initialization occurs. Right-click on the feedback node and configure the node to **Initailize On First Call**; refer to the following screenshot. The **Initailize On First Call** option will cause the feedback node to initialize when it is executed for the first time in a program. The **Initialize On Compile Or Load** option will cause the feedback node to initialize when the program containing the feedback node is first loaded in memory, that is, after we open the VI, the feedback node will initialize one time. After that, it does not matter how many times we start or stop the program, the feedback node will not initialize.

3. To achieve the same functionality of the preceding program with a shift register, refer to the following screenshot. It contains a while loop, since a shift register can only be created within a while loop or a for loop. The shift register is uninitialized, which means a value is not wired to the left shift register. In that case, the shift register will initialize to the default value of that data type, which is **I32** in our example. To find out what the default value of a particular data type is, just right-click on a control, indicator, shift register, and so on of that data type and create a constant. The constant will contain the default value of that type. Within the while loop, it contains a case structure that will wire out a **0** at its true case. For the false case, the input and output are connected directly.

To achieve the same functionality as the feedback node, the initialization scheme contains more code for the shift register approach.

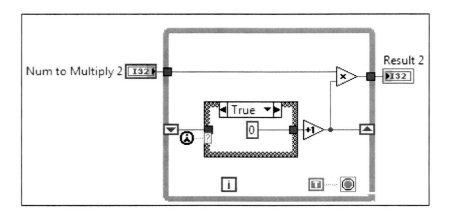

How it works...

The feedback node is similar to a shift register, but it does not require a loop and it has different initialization options. To initialize a shift register, a value can be wired to its input so that the shift register initializes every time it runs; custom initialization logic can also be used to initialize the shift register. For example, in an action engine, it can have an action dedicated to initialize the shift register. For the feedback node, there are two initialization options: **Initialize On Compile Or Load** and **Initialize On First Call**. If the feedback loop is inside a loop, another initialization option, **Move Initializer One Loop Out**, is present. This option is very similar to wiring a value to a shift register for initialization.

Reusing memory

To keep memory usage manageable, it is desirable to declare a chunk of memory for reuse. LabVIEW does memory management automatically. However, for very large array, extra caution is required to ensure that memory usage is efficient. In this recipe, we will develop a timer array action engine.

How to do it...

To create an action engine, we start by placing a while loop on a block diagram and place a case structure within the loop.

1. In the action engine, the **Initialize** case will create a user-specified number of data value references with the new data value reference node in a for loop. The created references are saved in a shift register as an array, as shown in the following screenshot:

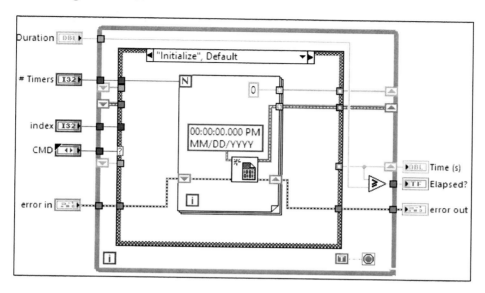

2. The second case of the action engine implements the **Start Timer** and **Unpause Timer** commands. It puts the current timestamp to the reference of the specified index. The **In Place Element Structure** is used. It operates the values of memory locations in place without allocating extra memory, as shown in the following screenshot:

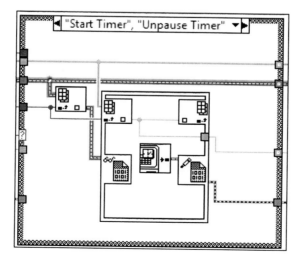

3. The next case of the action engine calculates elapsed time. It subtracts the current timestamp from the stored timestamp to obtain elapsed time and adds it to the total elapsed time.

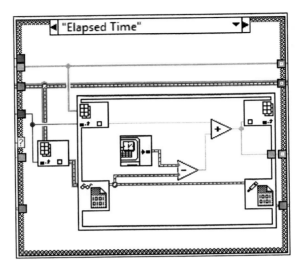

4. The next case of the action engine pauses the timer by storing the current elapsed time to the total elapsed time, as shown in the following diagram:

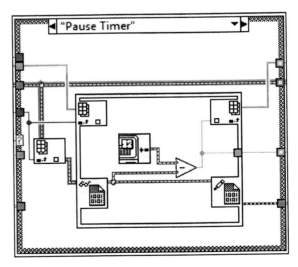

5. The last case of the action engine is **"Shutdown"**. It closes all the data references created for the timers in a for loop:

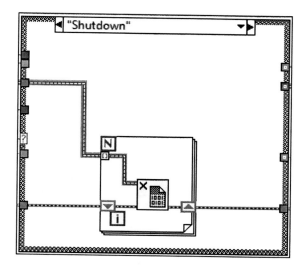

How it works...

This action engine uses data reference to modify data in place with the **In Place Element Structure**. To use the action engine, the user would first initialize how many timers are needed and create the corresponding number of data references that are saved in a shift register for later retrieval. After the timers are initialized, the user can use the **Start Timer** command to save the start time into the specified data reference. After the timer is started, the user can use the **Pause Timer** command to pause the timer, which will save the current elapsed time into the shift register for total elapsed time. To unpause timer, the user issues the **Unpause Timer** command, which would overwrite the start timestamp with the current timestamp. The **Shutdown** command will clear all data references used for the timers.

Manipulating an array

Manipulating array improperly could be memory costly. This recipe demonstrates how to manipulate array properly.

How to do it...

We will start by demonstrating how to add an element in front of an array efficiently.

1. Create the following block diagram to insert an element in front of an array. At the top of the block diagram, use the build array node directly to add an element in the beginning of an array. At the bottom of the block diagram, we see reversal of the array, addition of the element, and reversal of the array again. The later approach is more memory efficient, since no additional memory allocation is required. Reversing the array only requires pointers change. When memory is allocated for an array, extra memory is available at the end of the allocated memory, so adding an element to the end of an array does not require additional memory allocation.

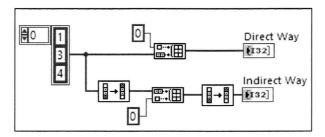

2. Build the block diagram as shown in the following screenshot. At the top of the diagram, the second element of an array is multiplied by two. At the bottom of the block diagram, an array is divided into two arrays at length 1. Both arrays are multiplied by 2 and 3 respectively and combined back together into one array.

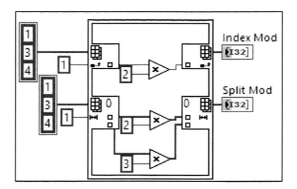

How it works...

While inserting an element in front of an array, if it is done directly, memory is reallocated. Instead, if the element is inserted in the front of the array by reversing the array, appending the element to the end of the array, and reversing the array once more, memory is not reallocated, so it is more efficient. Reversing an array doesn't require memory reallocation, since only pointers are changing.

Using rendezvous

The rendezvous ensures that a section of code is executed only if multiple threads of code are completed. In the following recipe, we will show an example of using the rendezvous.

How to do it...

We will create a program that uses rendezvous to synchronize three loops:

1. Create the following block diagram. It creates a rendezvous and feeds the reference into three while loops in parallel threads. The case structures in the while loops will execute its false case first, based on the initialized values of the shift registers. The loops will wait for 1, 2, and 3 seconds in parallel. When the wait time is done, the loops will display a string to indicate the status.

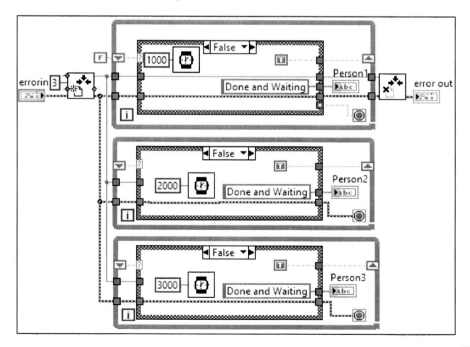

2. The true case is executed after the false case is executed, as shown in the following screenshot. The false case will wait for all the loops using the rendezvous. When all the loops have arrived, a string is outputted to indicate the status.

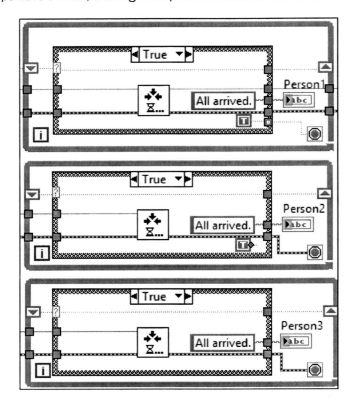

How it works...

The example creates a rendezvous for three while loops. Each loop waits for a different amount of time, and they will wait for each other before they output a string that indicates all has arrived. The rendezvous is used to synchronize multiple threads of a program by forcing different threads to wait for one another before proceeding.

Using semaphore

Semaphore is used to limit the number of tasks that can operate on a shared or protected resource. In this recipe, we demonstrate how the semaphore is used in a modified version of a cigarette smoker's problem, described by *S. S. Patil*.

How to do it...

The program will simulate three smokers manufacturing and smoking cigarette together. When a smoker is smoking, the smoker will be too busy to help, on smoke break.

1. Create the following block diagram. First, an array of three semaphores is created. A semaphore is randomly selected and the table string is updated accordingly. The check release semaphore SubVI will check the status of each semaphore and update the smoker string accordingly.

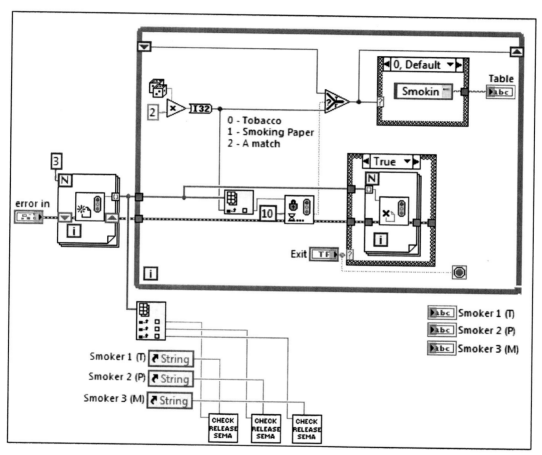

2. If the semaphore that a SubVI is responsible for is unavailable, the SubVI will update the smoker string to indicate its status and keep the status for 3 seconds before releasing the semaphore, as shown in the following screenshot:

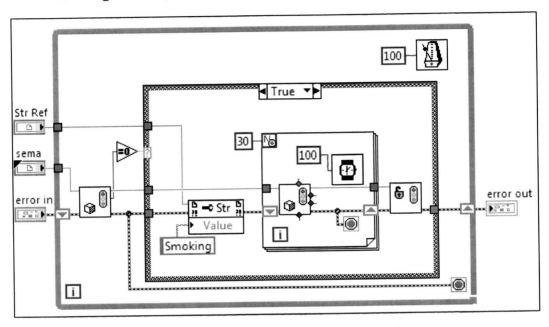

3. The front panel in the following screenshot shows how the program will update the status of the smokers and table:

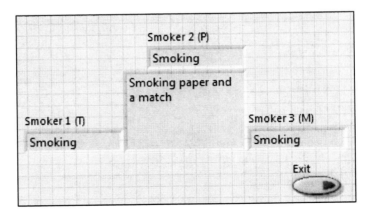

How it works...

In the program, three smokers are seated at a round table. One person has tobacco, one has smoking paper, and one has matches of an unlimited quantity. A material handler will randomly go to two smokers and put their supply on the table. The third smoker will take the supply from the table, and along with his supply, he will make a cigarette and smoke it. While he is smoking the cigarette, the material handler can take the smoker's supply. However, if there are supplies on the table for him to make another cigarette, but he is smoking, he will wait until he finishes his cigarette.

The example creates three semaphores, one for each smoker, and randomly selects one to make the cigarette by taking the semaphore. The SubVI will check for the status of each semaphore in parallel. If a semaphore is unavailable, the smoker will start smoking for 3 seconds and release the semaphore.

See also

▶ For more details on the cigarette smokers' problems, refer to
http://en.wikipedia.org/wiki/Cigarette_smokers_problem

5
Passing Data

In this chapter, we will cover:

- ▸ Using a type-def cluster
- ▸ Using an event structure to pass data
- ▸ Using a queue to pass data
- ▸ Using a notifier to pass data
- ▸ Using a shared variable to pass data
- ▸ Using Simple TCP/IP Messaging to pass data

Introduction

This chapter presents tips on passing data in LabVIEW. Cluster, event structure, queue, notifier, shared variable, and Simple TCP/IP Messaging (STM) are the ways of passing data that we will discuss in this chapter.

Using a type-def cluster

A cluster is like an array, but a cluster can contain elements of different data types. A type-def control is a centralized control that propagates its changes to the associated controls in the program. A cluster is usually created as a type-def control to avoid rework, and it is used to pass data in a program. It is a great way to anticipate data structure changes in the future. If the appearance of the type-def needs to be preserved, with respect to the exact placement of each element, a type-def should be made into a strict type-def. In this recipe, we will create a program that passes data with a type-def cluster.

How to do it...

We will create a state machine that uses a cluster to pass data from one state to the next.

1. Create a type-def cluster that we will be using to pass data from one state to another within the state machine. In a block diagram, navigate to **File | New... | Custom Control**. A front panel will appear. Drop a cluster on the front panel and populate the cluster with elements. Note that the label of each element will be used to bundle and unbundle elements from the cluster. See the following screenshot for the cluster. The cluster contains three floating point values and a string.

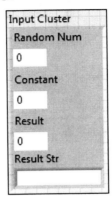

2. Build the following state machine. Outside the while loop, place a type-def cluster with three floating point numbers (**Random Num**, **Constant**, and **Result**) and a string (**Result Str**). A type-def enum feeding the state shift register from outside of the while loop will initialize the state machine to start at that state. The enum contains all the states of the machine. The **Initialize** state is also the default state. If an input of the case structure is unaccounted for, this state is executed. This state bundles the **Constant** input onto the cluster, passes the cluster to the next state, and goes to the **Generate Number** state.

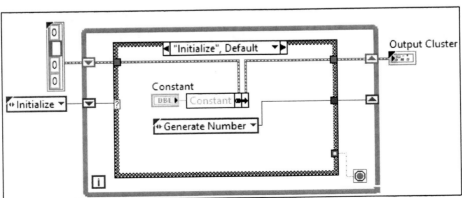

3. The next state is **"Generate Number"**. It generates a random number from 0 to 1, bundles the value onto the cluster, and goes to the next state, as shown in the following screenshot:

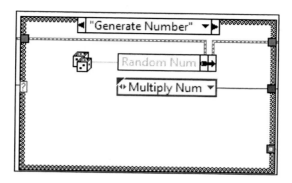

4. The next state is the **"Multiply Num"** state. It unbundles values **Random Num** and **Constant** from the cluster, multiplies them, and bundles the result onto the cluster under **Result**, as shown in the following screenshot:

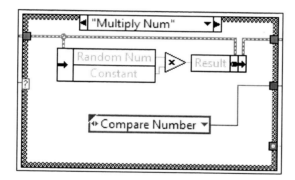

5. The next state is the **"Compare Number"** state. It unbundles **Result** from the cluster and feeds the value into a case structure. The **Default** case is executed when the input value does not match any condition from the other cases. In this case, the string **>50** is outputted and bundled onto the cluster under **Result Str**, as shown in the following screenshot:

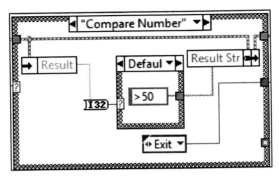

6. The following screenshot shows the other case of the case structure. If the input is less than or equal to 50, the string **<=50** is output.

7. The last state is the **"Exit"** state. It sets the stop condition of the state machine to `true`. The state machine will exit in this state.

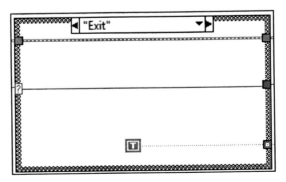

How it works...

This recipe uses a state machine. To use the state machine, a cluster for data passing and an enum with all states are created. The machine starts with the **Initialize** state, in which the user input **Constant** is bundled into the cluster and passed to the next state **Generate Number**. In the next state, a random number is generated and bundled into the cluster before going to the **Multiply Num** state. In the **Multiply Num** state, **Random Num** and **Constant** are unbundled from the cluster and multiplied. The result is bundled onto the cluster **Result** and passed to the next state **Compare Number**. In the next state, **Result Str** is created and bundled onto the cluster based on the value of **Result**. At the end, the machine transits to the last state, **Exit**, where the state machine is shutdown. Instead of using local and global variables to pass data, using a cluster is the main way in LabVIEW to pass data. Since only one data structure, the cluster, is used to pass data, the code is very organized, and it follows the data flow structure of LabVIEW.

Using an event structure to pass data

An event structure executes when events occur. When there is no event, event structures sit idle, consuming no CPU resource, contrary to a while loop, which will execute constantly to poll for events. In addition to executing code based on actual events, it can execute code based on a software event (user event) that is triggered within the software. A user event can also be used to pass data. This recipe demonstrates how to pass data to an event structure.

How to do it...

In this example, we will create a program that passes data between loops based on user events.

1. Place the `Create User Event` and `Register For Events` functions on the block diagram to create and register an user event. See the following screenshot:

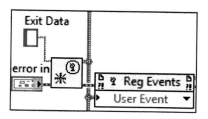

2. The Event Registration Refnum from the `Register for Event` node is fed into the Dynamic Event Terminal of the event structure in the top loop. The User Event Refnum from the `Create User Event` node is fed into the bottom loop to generate a user event. The top loop contains an event structure to handle events, and the bottom loop is a state machine that implements a task. The **"Cheese": Value Change** event case is executed when the **Cheese** Boolean control is clicked on, and it would output the string **Cheese**. The **Initialize** case at the bottom loop initializes values of the program. See the following screenshot:

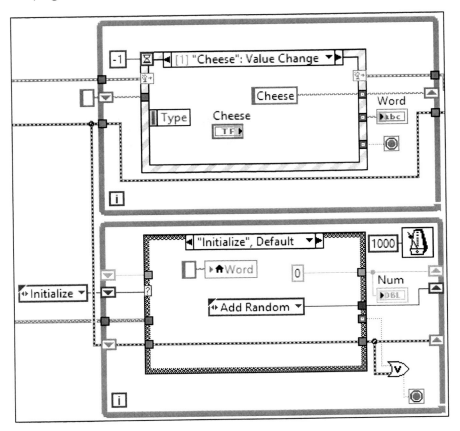

3. In the top loop, the next event case is **"Hello": Value Change**. It is executed when the **Hello** Boolean control is clicked on, and the string **Hello** is outputted, as shown in the following screenshot:

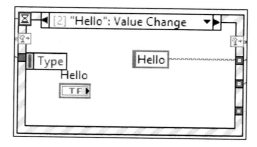

4. In the top loop, the next event case is **"Exit": Value Change**. It is executed when the **Exit** Boolean control is clicked on. It outputs the **Exit without data** string and sets the stop condition of the top loop to **true**.

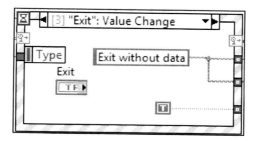

5. In the last event case, it is the <**Exit Data>: User Event** case. It is executed when a software-based user event is generated. It compares **Exit Data** that is passed from the bottom loop, where the user event is generated with the string **check**. If the string passed is not equal to **check**, the string from **Exit Data** is outputted. Otherwise, the string in the top loop shift register is passed.

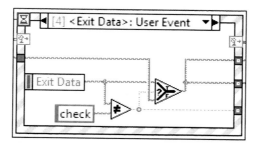

6. In the bottom loop, the next case is **"Add Random"**. It generates a random number, multiplies it by 1.1, and adds it to the value in the shift register.

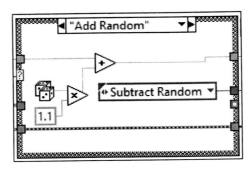

7. For the bottom loop, the next case is **"Subtract Random"**. It generates a random number and subtracts it from the value in the shift register.

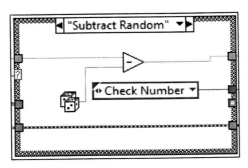

8. For the bottom loop, the next case is **"Check Number"**. It compares the value within the shift register with the **Stop Limit** floating point number specified by users on the front panel. If the value of the shift register is greater than **Stop Limit**, the next state is **Exit**. Otherwise, the next state is **Add Random**. A user event is also generated to pass the string **check** to the top loop. When the top loop gets the string **check**, it will know that it does not have to exit.

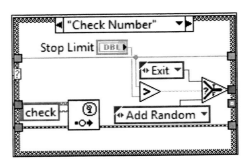

9. For the bottom loop, the last case is **"Exit"**. It creates the string **Exit with Num %0.2f**, with **0.2f** being the input floating point number with two decimal points. The string is sent to the top loop through a user event. When the top loop recognizes that the string is not **check**, it will exit. The stop condition is also set to `true` to stop the loop.

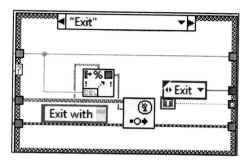

10. Outside the top loop, place `Unregister for Events` and `Destroy User Event`. They are used to free up resources occupied by references created that are no longer needed.

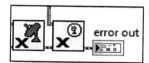

How it works...

This recipe contains two loops. The top loop handles events and displays a string accordingly. The bottom loop, starting from zero, adds and subtracts a random number until the result reaches a user-specified limit. Once the limit is reached, it uses user events to send the result to the top loop in a string.

When the user event is created with the `Create User Event` node, the name of the user event data type input becomes the name of the user event. The user event case is activated by the bottom loop every time when the bottom loop enters the **Check Number** or **Exit** state. When the bottom loop enters the **Check Number** state, a **check** string is passed to the top loop, and it signals the top loop to display previous values. When the **check** string is not sent, the top loop will update the string indicator with a new string.

In this example, the user event is used to synchronize the exit behavior of both loops. This is very important, since if one loop is terminated and the other one is not, the program will not exit, as a loop is still running. When the top loop is terminated first, the user event is unregistered and destroyed. When the bottom loop tries to generate a user event, an error will occur, since the event is no longer available. The bottom loop will stop as well. When the bottom loop is terminated first, a string that is not **check** is passed to the top loop. When the top loops recognize that the string passed is not **check**, it will exit.

Using a queue to pass data

This recipe shows you how to use a queue to pass data between loops. In a queue, data is preserved, unless the element is enqueued when the maximum number of elements is reached for the queue and time allocated to wait for an available space is up. In that case, data is lost.

How to do it...

We will create a program that generates waveform data in one loop and passes it to another to display the data.

1. Create a queue with name **Wave**, 100 elements, and double data type. The queue will have the capacity to hold 100 floating point numbers.

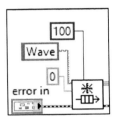

2. Create two while loops. The top loop contains an event structure. The **Timeout** event case is executed once every 100 ms. It generates one point on a sine wave and enqueues the data. To enqueue data means putting data on a queue. The bottom loop dequeues the data and puts it on a chart once every 1000 ms. To dequeue data means taking data off a queue. See the following screenshot. Note that data is going on the queue faster than going off. Since the timeout terminal is not wired, the enqueue operation will never timed out by default. When the `enqueue` node is executed and the queue is full, the program will pause at the `enqueue` node until a space is available by a dequeue operation.

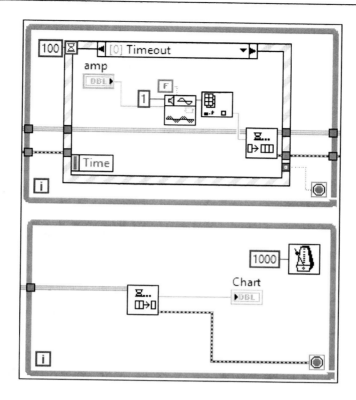

3. The next event case in the top loop is **Exit**. It is executed when the **Exit** Boolean control is clicked on. It sets the stop condition of the while loop to the value of the **Exit** Boolean control, which will be `true` and cause the loop to exit.

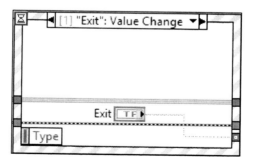

4. Outside the loop, the queue reference is destroyed. This is located outside of the top loop. When the queue reference is destroyed, the bottom loop will exit as well, since the stop condition of the bottom loop is wired with the error terminal of the `dequeue` node. When the queue reference is destroyed, the `dequeue` node will generate an error, which will cause the bottom loop to stop.

How it works...

This recipe contains two loops. The top loop generates a data point of a sine wave once every 100 ms. The data is passed to the bottom loop via a queue. The bottom loop dequeues the data and displays it on a chart once every one second. Once the user clicks on exit, the top loop is completed, and the `destroy queue` function is executed. At that point, the queue reference becomes invalid. When the bottom loop tries to dequeue an element with an invalid queue reference, an error occurs and it will stop the bottom loop. When the program enqueues an element to the queue and the queue is full, the program will get stuck at the `enqueue` node until an element is dequeued to free up a space, since no timeout is specified.

Using a notifier to pass data

A notifier allows for passing the same piece of data to multiple locations, contrary to a queue. This recipe demonstrates how to use the notifier to pass data.

How to do it...

We will create a program that passes a user-specified amplitude to two different loops that generate a sine and triangular wave.

1. Place the `Obtain Notifier` node with a double precision number as element data type input.

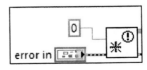

2. Create three while loops. The top loop contains an event structure that is executed after the loop is executed once, which is when the `First Call?` function outputs false. When a notification is received in the bottom loops, the `Wait on Notification` node receives the new amplitude from the top loop and generates a data point on the sine and triangular waves accordingly. The new amplitude is saved in the shift register. Without getting a notification form the top loop, the `Wait on Notification` node in the bottom loops will time out in 5 ms to generate points of a sine and triangular wave to display them with the previous amplitude stored in the shift register.

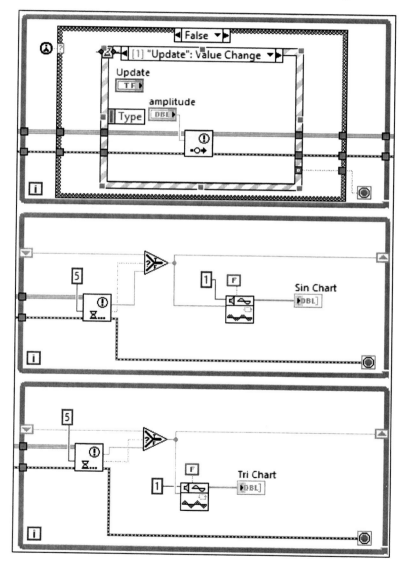

3. For the top loop, the true case notifies the bottom loops of the initial amplitude when the program starts.

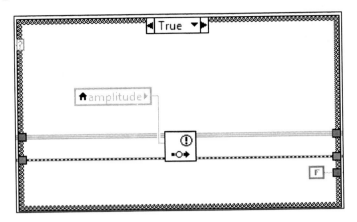

4. The next event case of the top loop handles when the **Exit** button is clicked, as shown in the following screenshot:

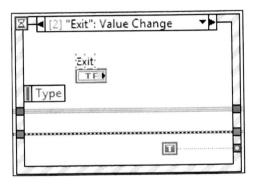

5. When the top loop exits, it proceeds to the `Destroy Notifier` node. After the notifier is destroyed, the bottom loops, which wait for the notifier, will generate an error, since the notifier is no longer available. The error will cause the bottom loops to exit.

How it works...

The recipe generates sinusoidal and triangular waves based on user-specified amplitude. When a user clicks on update, the amplitude is sent to the bottom loops through a notifier. The bottom loops will use the new amplitude to generate the waves accordingly. If the bottom loops do not get a new amplitude in 5 ms, the `Wait on Notification` node will timeout and the bottom loops will use the previous amplitude to generate the waves. Once the user clicks on exit, the top loop will be completed and execute Release Notification, which will invalidate the notifier's reference. When the bottom loops wait for a notification with an invalid reference, errors occur and the loops are stopped.

Using a shared variable to pass data

A shared variable is used to pass data within a program, among different programs on the same PC, and among programs that are deployed in different PCs within the same network. It is very similar to a global variable, but contains features that can prevent racing condition. This recipe demonstrates how to use shared variables to pass data.

How to do it...

We will create two VIs that run on the same PC that share data with a shared variable. This variable type is called "single process". For a variable that is accessible to all PCs across the same network, the variable type is called "network publish".

1. Create a project. Right-click on **My Computer**, and navigate to **New | Variable**. When a dialog box appears, configure the variable to single process. See the following screenshot to know how the project looks like after the variable is added.

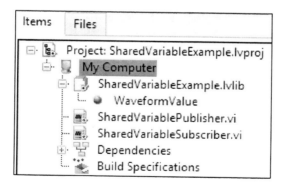

2. Create the following block diagram. This acts as a server. It generates a point on a sine wave with random amplitude and writes it to the shared variable `WaveformValue` once every 500 ms. A user can stop the loop by clicking the **stop** Boolean control.

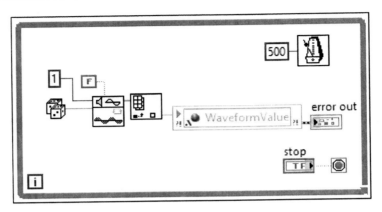

3. Create the following block diagram. This is a separate VI, and it acts as a client. It reads the `WaveformValue` node and the timestamp when the value was written. This is executed once every 100 ms. A user can click on the **stop** Boolean control to stop the loop.

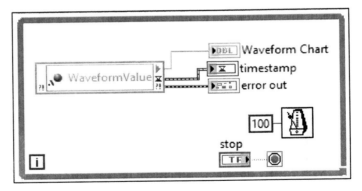

How it works...

In this recipe, we created a single process shared variable. It is used like a global variable in this recipe; the server and client VI are both on the same workstation. Shared variables can also be configured in such a way that they can be accessed by any computer on the same network. In this recipe, the server generates a data point on a sinusoidal wave and the client gets the data and displays it on a chart. The timestamp information is also displayed in the client, and it reflects when the new value is written to the variable.

Using Simple TCP/IP Messaging to pass data

Simple TCP/IP Messaging (**STM**) is another way to pass data between programs within a PC and programs running on different PCs on the same network. It is very similar to the shared variable, but uses the TCP/IP protocol for communication. This recipe demonstrates how to use STM to pass data.

How to do it...

In this example, we will create two programs that reside on the same PC, and they will communicate via STM.

1. Create the server VI. The first state is **Initialize**. It waits for a TCP connection at port **55555** and sets up variable name for the connection. It sets up the metadata for messaging, which is then sent to the other side for message decoding purposes. The name of the variable **Number** is sent as the metadata. Since STM is communicating via TCP/IP, firewall could present a problem for the communication. If that's the case, make exception for the port where the communication takes place in the PC network setup. Consult an IT professional for the configuration. See the following screenshot:

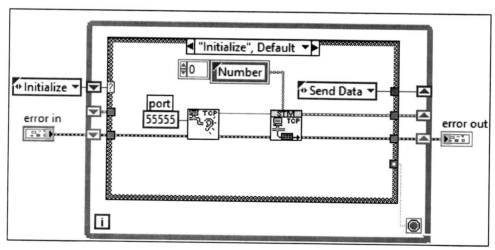

2. The next state is **"Send Data"**. It contains an event structure. The **"Send": Value Change** event case is executed when a user clicks on **Send**. It will send the user-specified **Number** through the network. The number sent is specified by the user through the control on the front panel. See the following screenshot:

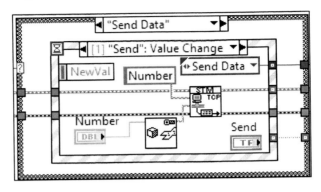

3. The next event case is **stop**. It will transition the program to the **Exit** state, as shown in the following screenshot:

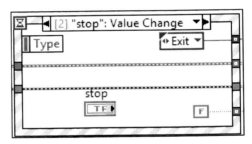

4. The next state is **"Exit"**. It gets the TCP reference and closes it.

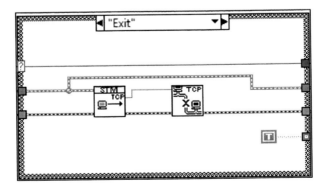

5. Create the client VI. It is a state machine. In the first state **Initialize**, it makes a TCP/IP connection to **localhost** (itself) at port **55555** and reads the metadata for message decoding purposes, as shown in the following screenshot:

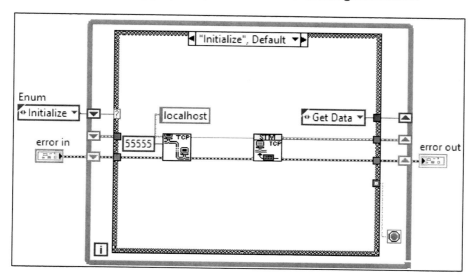

6. The next state is **"Get Data"**. It reads the actual data that is described by the metadata and interprets it. When the STM Read Message node is not timed out, a value is received. If the value has the metadata **Number**, which is what is expected, the received string will be unflattened into a double-precision value. If the **Exit** Boolean control is clicked on, the state machine transitions into the **Exit** state. If not, the state machine will go to the **Get Data** state.

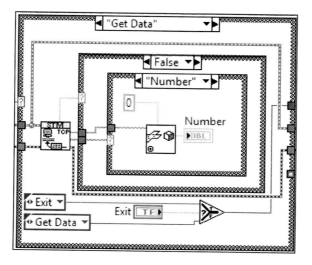

7. The next state is **"Exit"**. See the following screenshot. It closes all the references that were created. It sets the stop condition of the state machine to `true` to stop the loop.

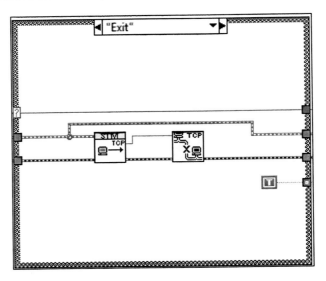

How it works...

In this recipe, there is a server VI and a client VI. The server VI waits for the client VI to establish a connection and transmits the metadata to the client once the connection is made. The client will receive data every time the server clicks on send.

See also

▶ LabVIEW does not come with the Simple TCP/IP Message (STM) library. Please download `stm_202_installer.zip` from the following link for installer files: `http://zone.ni.com/devzone/cda/epd/p/id/2739`. After installation, you can access STM through the palette under **User Libraries**.

6
Error Handling

In this chapter, we will cover:

- ▶ Passing an error
- ▶ Handling an error with an error file
- ▶ Handling an error with a centralized VI
- ▶ Creating an error queue

Introduction

This chapter presents tips on different ways of handling errors properly. This topic is often ignored, since LabVIEW can handle some errors automatically. However, designing our own error handling scheme will make debugging much easier, since we can add custom error information, logging, and so on to facilitate the debugging process.

Passing an error

This recipe demonstrates how an error is passed within a state machine. When an error occurs, it should bypass all subsequent code, so that the error information is not corrupted. The error information will finally arrive at an error handler that will show a dialog, log the error in a file, and so on.

How to do it...

We will create a state machine with states that will generate an error at random. When an error occurs, it will pass it to the error handling state and the error handler will cause an error dialog to appear.

1. Create the state machine in the following block diagram. The enum is a type-def with values **Case 1**, **Case 2**, **Case 3**, and **End**. All cases, except for **Case 3** and **End** case, call `GenerateError.vi` and transit to the next state. We will look into the SubVI in later steps.

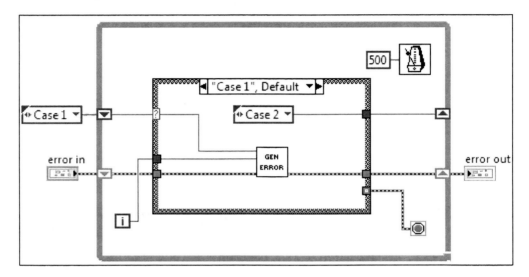

2. Case 2 is almost identical to Case 1, so it is not shown. The only difference is that Case 2 will transition to Case 3 instead. For **Case 3**, the same SubVI is called, but if an error has occurred, the next state is **End**; if not, the state machine goes back to **Case 1**.

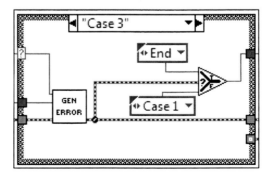

3. For the **"End"** case, see the following screenshot. The error is handled by the **Simple Error Handler**. If there is an error, it will cause an error dialog to appear to indicate that an error has occurred.

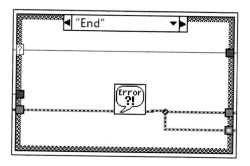

4. The SubVIs used in Cases 1, 2, and 3 are shown in the following screenshot. If an error happens upstream, the **Error** case (not shown) is executed. The case doesn't do much, it only passes the error from the upstream through without corrupting it. For the **No Error** case, the inputs `Numeric` and `State` are used to make the error message more descriptive, so that we know when and where an error occurs. It randomly generates an error by comparing a random number with the number 0.8. If the random number is greater than 0.8, an error is created. It creates an error message that indicates at what state and what iteration the error has occurred. All errors get the error code 5000. In LabVIEW, the custom error code ranges are -8999 through -8000, 5000 through 9999, and 500,000 through 599,999. We pick 5000 for simplicity, but we can make the error code as an input and make the error generated by each state to have a different code. The error and false cases are blank while feeding through the applicable terminals. There are error codes that are used by LabVIEW. To find more information on these codes, visit `http://zone.ni.com/ reference/en-XX/help/371361J-01/lverror/misc_lv_error_codes/`.

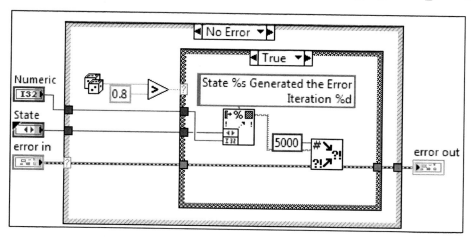

How it works...

In this example, an error is generated randomly if a random number is greater than 0.8. In the SubVI, an error case structure encloses all the code so that the code is bypassed if there is an error upstream. This is an important aspect in error passing/handling. If an error occurs, it should jump over all the subsequent code so that the error information is not corrupted, and the error is handled downstream at a designated portion of the code.

Cases 1 to 3 generate an error at random. At **Case 3**, if no error has occurred, the program will go back to **Case 1**. If an error has occurred, the program will go to the **End** state. In the **End** state, the Simple Error Handler will generate a dialog that notifies the user of the error.

Handling an error with an error file

This recipe demonstrates how to handle errors through one central file. The file is text-based and can be read without LabVIEW. The exact wording of the error can be updated easily, and every error that is handled is clearly seen. When an application that uses an error file is deployed, the error file must be deployed with the application as well.

How to do it...

The last example created both the error message and error code within the program. In this example, the error code is still specified within the program, but the error message is captured inside a text file.

1. In this example, we will use the state machine in the previous recipe, *Passing an error*. Only the SubVI will be modified. Do a `Save As` on the previous recipe and save it as another name.

2. The SubVI will randomly generate an error. The random number is converted to integers between 5000-5009. The error code is converted to an error cluster through the `Error Cluster From Error Code` VI.

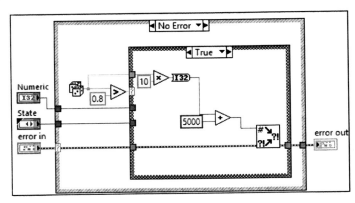

3. Create an error file that associates error code to error description. In the block diagram, navigate to **Tools | Advanced | Edit Error Codes**. Create a new error file and save it in the `<version>\user.lib\errors` folder. The format of the error file's name is `xxx-errors.txt`, where `xxx` is the name of the file.

Range Name (non-localized n
ErrorFile

Range Display Name (localize
ErrorFile

Comments about this file

Errors

Code	Text
5000	Level 0 Error
5001	Level 1 Error
5002	Level 2 Error
5003	Level 3 Error
5004	Level 4 Error
5005	Level 5 Error

How it works...

Similar to the previous recipe, *Passing an error*, this example generates an error at random. The difference is how the error information is packaged. In the previous recipe, the error information is packaged inside the code. For this recipe, the error information is located in an error file, and the code can extract information by using the corresponding error code. This is a good method for centralizing error information, but it creates an additional file that must be deployed properly at deployment time.

See also

When deploying an executable, the location of the error file associated with the executable is different from the location of the file in development mode. For more information, refer to the following link: http://www.ni.com/white-paper/3209/en/.

Handling an error with a centralized VI

This recipe demonstrates how to group all the error information in a VI. With this approach, all error information is within one VI, and there is no need to keep track of an error file.

How to do it...

We will create a state machine that will generate an error randomly. When the error is generated, it will bypass subsequent code and go to the error handler.

1. Build the state machine as shown in the following screenshot. The enum is a type-def and it has the **Initialize**, **Case 1**, **Case 2**, **Case 3**, and **End** values. The **Initialize** case sends all the possible error codes and messages into SubVI for handling.

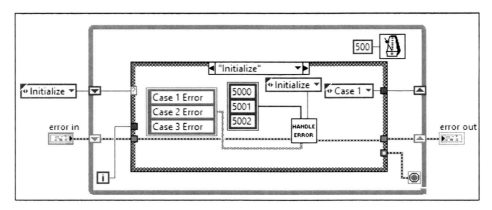

2. **Case 1** uses a SubVI to generate an error at random.

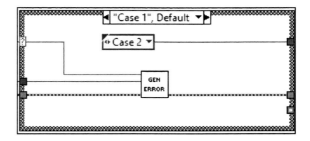

3. **Case 2** is almost identical to Case 1, except that Case 2 transitions to Case 3, so the screenshot for Case 2 is not shown. **Case 3** would transit back to **Case 1** if there is no error. It would transit to the **End** state if an error has occurred. See the following screenshot:

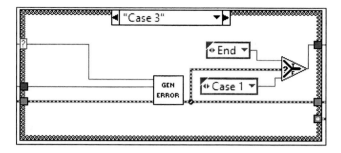

4. The **"End"** state calls a SubVI to handle the error.

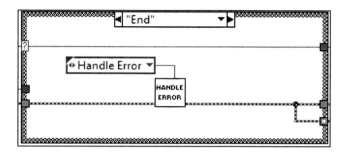

5. The error handling SubVI is shown in the following screenshot. The **Initialize** state saves the error information into shift registers.

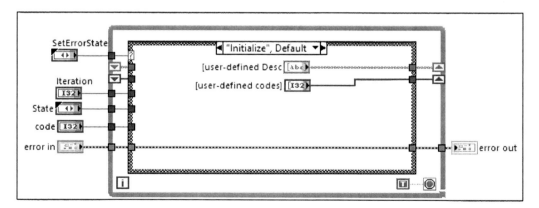

6. The second state of the error handling SubVI handles the error.

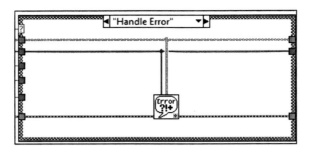

7. The SubVI that generates errors at random is shown in the following screenshot. The inputs Numeric and State are used to make the error message more descriptive, so that we know when and where an error occurs. It randomly generates an error by comparing a random number with the number 0.8. If the random number is greater than 0.8, an error is created. It gives the error a message that indicates at what state and what iteration the error had occurred. The `Format Into String` node is used to create an error message with the given inputs. A different error code is given depending on what state the error had occurred. An error code is associated with the error cluster depending on which case the error occurred in.

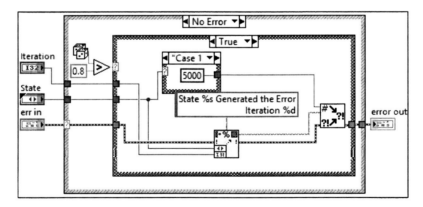

How it works...

This example shows how to consolidate error information and put it inside the code. By doing that, error information is centralized without having to use an error file. In the example, the first case saves all the error information into the error handler SubVI. To make the program more elegant, we can create a wrapper VI around it. After the **Initialize** state the program will generate an error randomly. In **Case 3**, the program will go to the **End** state, if an error has occurred. If not, the program will go back to **Case 1**. When the program arrives at the **End** state, it means an error has occurred, and it will be handled by the error handling SubVI.

Creating an error queue

This recipe demonstrates how to use an error queue in a parallel process for error handling. This allows for handling errors across multiple VIs.

How to do it...

For this error handling method, the error handling VI runs in the background of the main program to handle errors.

1. Build the state machine as shown in the following screenshot. The enum has the values of **Initialize**, **Case 1**, **Case 2**, **Case 3**, and **End**. The **Initialize** state builds a path for **BackError.vi**, assuming that the VI is in the same folder as the main VI and opens the VI reference with the `Open VI Reference` node. The reference is wired to an `Invoke Node` and the **Run VI** method is selected, which will call the VI dynamically in the background. Outside the case structure, if there is an error, a SubVI will send the error cluster to the background VI and change the main state to the **End** state.

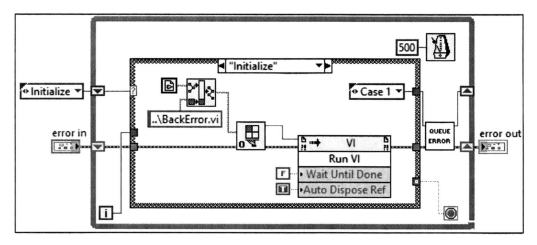

2. Cases 1, 2, and 3 will generate an error at random. They are identical. See the following screenshot for **Case 1**:

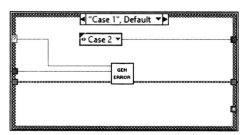

3. Case **"End"** terminates the queue that is used to pass data to the background VI.

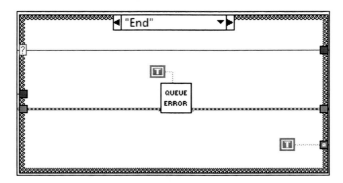

4. The queuing error SubVI is shown in the following screenshot. When an error occurs upstream and is passed into the SubVI, a reference to the error queue is obtained with the `Obtain Queue` node and the error cluster is enqueued with the `Enqueue Element` node. Refer to *Chapter 3, Working with Common Architectures*, to see another application on how a queue is used.

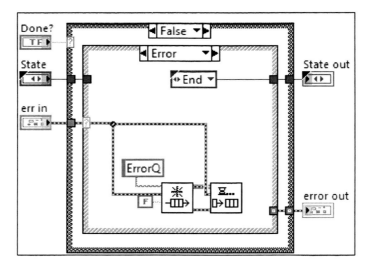

5. In the error queuing SubVI, when the **Done?** Boolean is set to **True**, the reference of the error queue is obtained and released. For the release queue function, be sure to set force destroy to **True**, since many references of the queue exist.

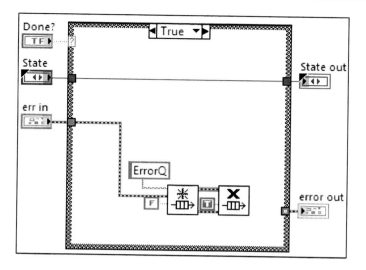

6. The true cases of the background error VI are shown in the following screenshot. When the VI is called for the first time, the true cases are executed. It creates an `Error.txt` file in the same folder as the main VI, sets up error information with handle error SubVI, and obtains a reference for the error queue.

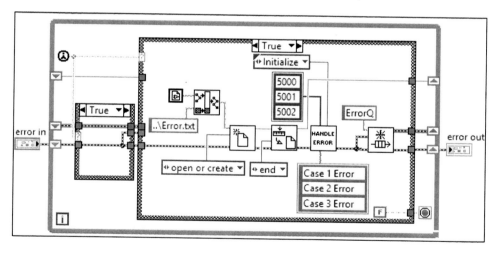

7. The false cases of the background error VI are shown in the following screenshot. They are executed when the VI is not executed for the first time. It waits for an element to dequeue indefinitely. When an element is available, it is dequeued and written into a file.

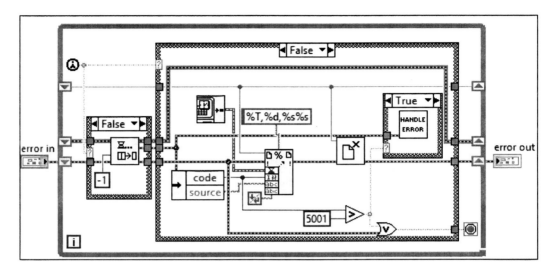

8. If the error code is greater than 5001, an error dialog will appear to alert the user of the error. See the following screenshot for the dialog:

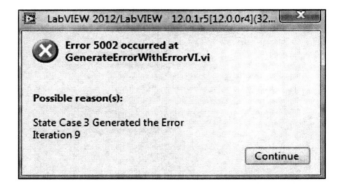

How it works...

This program consists of a main VI and a background VI. The main VI starts the background VI and generates an error at random. Once an error is generated, the main VI passes the error to the background VI through an error queue. Once the background VI receives the error information, it logs the information into a file. If the error code is greater than 5001, an error dialog will appear to signify the severity of the error.

7

Working with Files

In this chapter, we will cover the following recipes:

- ▸ Working with INI files
- ▸ Working with XML files
- ▸ Working with ASCII files
- ▸ Working with binary files
- ▸ Working with TDMS files
- ▸ Using Telnet and FTP with files
- ▸ Working with a database

Introduction

This chapter presents tips on working with different type of files, such as INI, XML, ASCII, binary, and TDMS. We will also explore how to use Telnet, FTP, and database in this chapter.

Working with INI files

An INI file is a configuration file that stores constants used in a program. The file consists of sections and keys. Keys are grouped in different sections. This recipe extracts the values from all keys within an INI file and stores them in a cluster so that the values can be retrieved within a program.

To read the values of all keys within an INI file, we create a state machine to iterate through the file, using following steps:

1. Create the INI file to read. See the following screenshot for the content within the INI file.

```
[Boolean Section]
Boolean1 = True
Boolean2 = True

[Double Section]
Double1 = 3.5
Double2 = 5.6

[I32 Section]
I32_1 = -3
I32_2 = 50023

[Path Section]
Path1 = c:\YEE_Automation

[String Section]
String1=Yik Yang
String2=YEE System Automation

[U32 Section]
U32_1 = 234234
U32_2 = 3087234

[Array Section]
Array1 = 3,4,2,3,5
Array2 = yik,yang,system,automation
```

2. Create a state machine, as shown in the following screenshot. It starts in the **Open INI** state to open an INI file located in the same folder as the VI. After this state is completed, it transits to the **Extract Values** state.

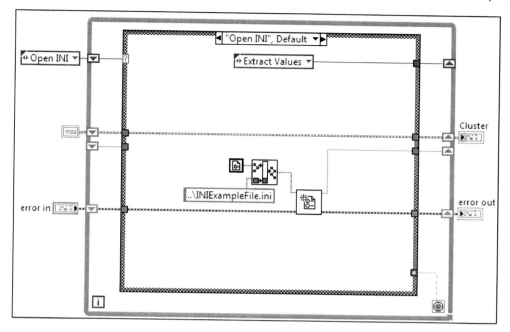

3. Create the **"Extract Values"** state, as shown in the following screenshot. It loops through all sections and keys in the INI file. The value of each key is bundled into a cluster.

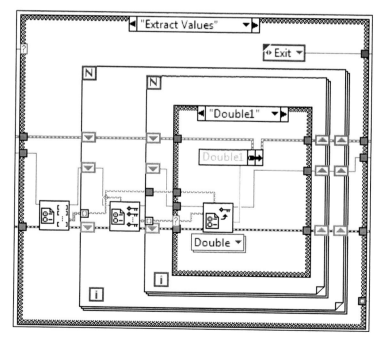

4. In the **Extract Values** state, it bundles the values of all the keys listed in the following picture into a cluster. The case structure takes string input, which is the name of the keys within the INI file.

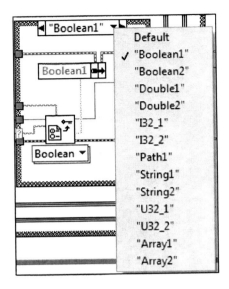

5. After all the values in the INI file are bundled into a cluster, the state machine transits to the **"Exit"** state. See the following screenshot, where the reference of the INI file is closed and error is handled:

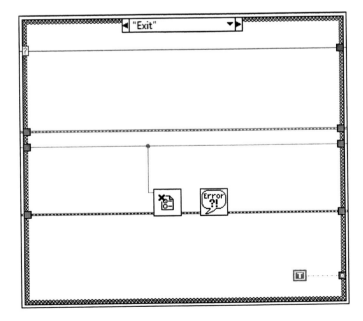

6. The cluster that the state machine populates is shown in the following screenshot:

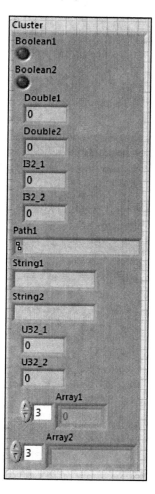

How it works...

This state machine reads an INI file in the same folder. It reads each section and key and stores all values into a cluster for further processing. Instead of hard coding the constants used directly into a program, using an INI file is the preferred way. If a value in the INI needs to be changed, the file can be opened, understood, and modified easily by any user. In contrast, if a value is hardcoded into a program, a code change is required. Furthermore, LabVIEW has built-in functions that work with an INI file, making use of INI files more convenient.

Working with XML files

Extensible Markup Language (**XML**) files store information in such a way that is both human and machine readable. In LabVIEW, there are many ways to work with XML, and this recipe presents a way to modify a value in an XML file.

How to do it...

In this example, we will create an XML file based on data of different people and write a LabVIEW application to modify a user-selected parameter in the file. This application comes in handy when you need to modify the same parameter on a thousand XML files. In that case, the application can be executed in a loop for all the files.

1. Create an XML file manually. The data for each person fall under student id. The name, gender, age, and company details for each person are recorded in the file. Have a look at the following screenshot:

```xml
<?xml version="1.0" encoding="UTF-8" standalone="no" ?>
- <record>
  - <student id="id01">
      <name>Yang, Yik</name>
      <gender>Male</gender>
      <age>32</age>
      <company>YEES</company>
    </student>
  - <student id="id02">
      <name>Smith, John</name>
      <gender>Male</gender>
      <age>14</age>
      <company>Missing</company>
    </student>
  </record>
```

2. Create the state machine, as shown in the following screenshot. The first state is **"User Input"**, which waits for users to click on **Start** or **Exit**. If a user clicks on **Start**, the machine populates a cluster with values from the front panel controls and goes to the **Initialize** state. If a user clicks on **Exit**, the machine transits to the **Close Ref** state immediately.

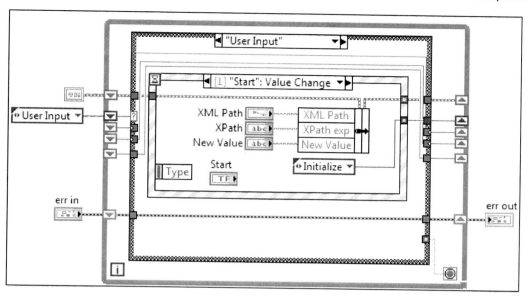

3. The next state is **"Initialize"**. It opens the XML file with a user-specified path and bundles the reference into the input cluster, as shown in the following screenshot:

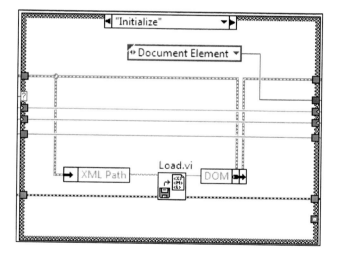

4. The next state is **"Document Element"**. It opens the reference of the element that is one level lower in the XML structure and transits to the next state **Match Node**.

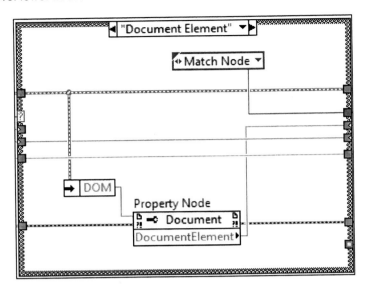

5. In the **"Match Node"** state, it takes an XPath expression (an XML search criteria) and returns a search result. Next, it transits to the **Child Node** state.

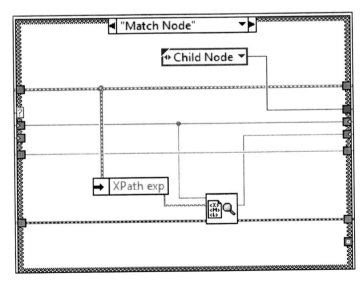

6. After the desired node is found, the **"Child Node"** state goes down one level in the XML structure and transits to the **Modify Value** state.

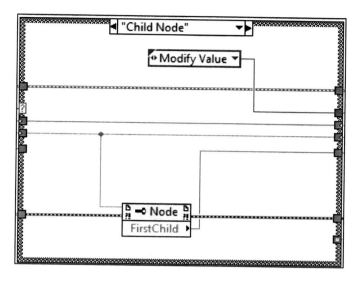

7. In the **"Modify Value"** state, it modifies a value based on user input and transits to the **Save XML** state, as shown in the following screenshot:

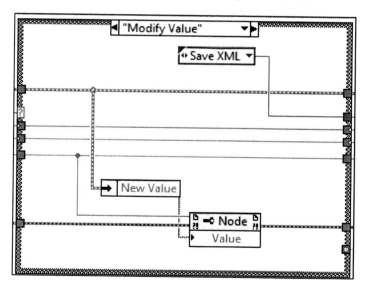

8. After changes are made to the XML file, the XML file is saved and transits to the
    Display XML state.

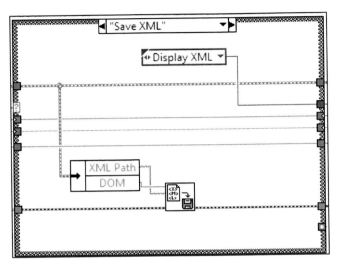

9. In the **"Display XML"** state, it reads the XML file and outputs the content into a string
    indicator. After that is done, it goes back to the **User Input** state to wait for the
    user's input.

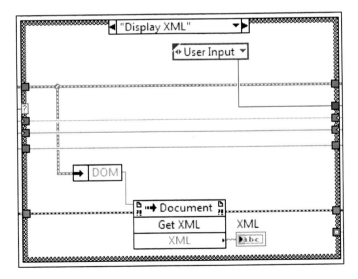

10. If the **Exit** button is clicked on, the **"Close Ref"** state is entered into. This state closes all XML references that are opened, as shown in the following screenshot:

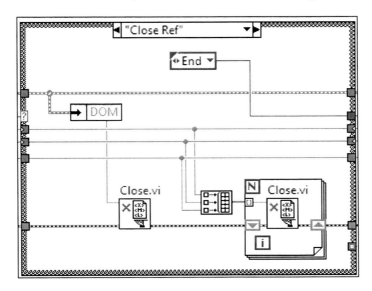

11. After references are closed, the program arrives to the **"End"** state where the program loop is stopped, as represented in the following screenshot:

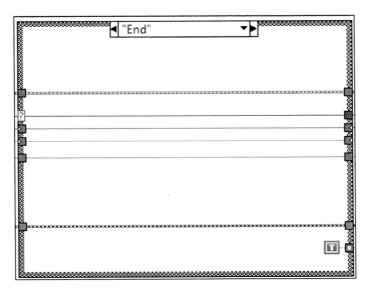

12. The front panel of the program is shown in the following screenshot. The user needs to enter the path of the XML file to be modified, the **XPath** expression, and **New Value** before clicking on **Start**.

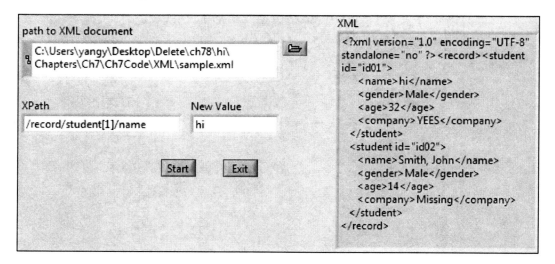

How it works...

The program searches for a value and modifies it. When a user clicks on **Start**, an XML file opens, goes down the XML structure to the desired node with an **XPath** search, and the associated value is modified. After the modification is done, the content of the XML is saved to the same file and displayed in the string indicator on the front panel. The user can continue to make changes to the XML file until the **Exit** button is clicked on.

See also

For more about XPath expression syntax, please refer to the link http://www.w3schools.com/xpath/xpath_syntax.asp.

There are more XML add-ons out there if you need more features or ease of use, check the following links:

► http://zone.ni.com/devzone/cda/epd/p/id/6330

► http://sine.ni.com/nips/cds/view/p/lang/en/nid/209021

Working with ASCII files

An ASCII file is simply a text file. In this recipe, we will create a text file with a header for multiple columns and random data underneath.

How to do it...

We will create a state machine to create and write in an ASCII file.

1. Create the state machine, as shown in the following screenshot. The first state is **Initialize**. It replaces or creates a `test.txt` text file in the same folder as the calling VI and passes the file reference to the next state. It also initializes the data point counter to 0 and data string with an empty string.

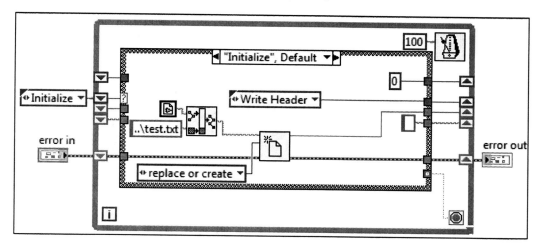

2. The next state is **"Write Header"**. It writes **Time, Data, Result** as header in the file. See the following screenshot for reference:

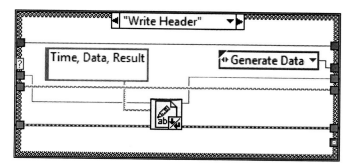

3. The next state is **"Generate Data"**. It generates a random number as test data with its status as **Pass** or **Fail**. If the random number is less than 0.5, the result is **Pass**, else it is **Fail**. The data and result are built into a string and passed into the next state.

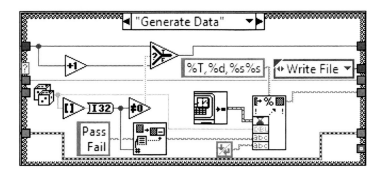

4. The next state is **"Write File"**. It writes the string generated by the previous state and then writes it into a file. If the data point counter is greater than 99, the program transits to the **End** state. If not, the program goes back to the **Generate Data** state for more data points.

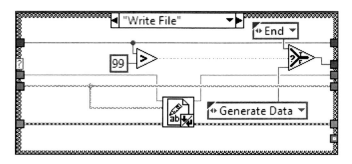

5. The last state is the **"End"** state. It closes the reference of the file and sets the stop condition of the state machine to true to exit the program.

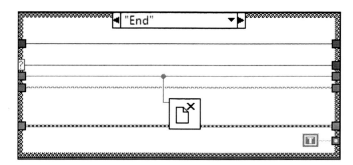

This recipe generates random numbers and puts them in an ASCII file. It creates or replaces a file and writes a header to it. A random number is generated. If it rounds down to zero, its result string is **Pass**. If it rounds up to one, its result string is **Fail**. With the random number and test result, a string is created and written into a text file. The process will continue until the number of test data is greater than 99. Once the limit is exceeded, the fail reference is closed and the program exits. In our example, the file is a txt file. If the file type is changed to **Comma Separated Value** (**CSV**) data type, it will recognize the data type and delimit the file properly whenever the file is opened in Excel.

Working with binary files

A binary file contains ones and zeroes. It is not human readable, unless the reader is Neo (there is no spoon). A binary file is used due to its small size and for security. This recipe demonstrates how to read and write to a binary file.

How to do it...

We will use a state machine to read/write to a binary file.

1. Build the state machine, as shown in the following screenshot. The first state is **Initialize**. It opens or creates an extensionless file called `test` in the same folder as calling VI. Next, it goes to the **User Input** state.

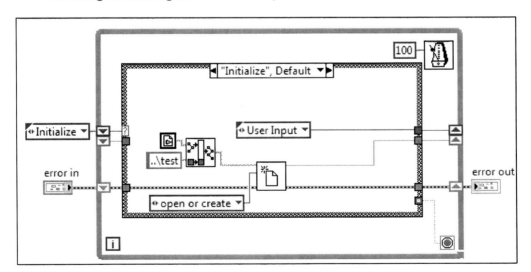

2. The next state is **"User Input"**. It waits for users to click on the **Read, Write,** or **Exit** button and transit to the corresponding state. See the following screenshot for your reference:

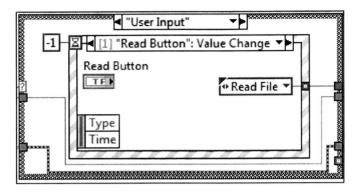

3. If the **Write** button is clicked on, the program transits into the **"Write File"** state. It writes an I16 array into the binary file with little-endian format and closes the file reference. Afterwards, the program goes back to the **Initialize** state, as represented in the following screenshot:

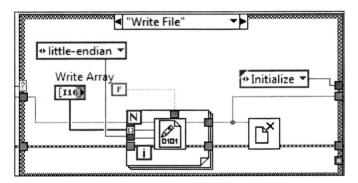

4. If the **Read** button is clicked on, the program transits into the **"Read File"** state. It determines the size of the binary file in bytes and divides it by 2 to find out how many I16 numbers are contained in the file. After the program determines how many I16 numbers are in the file, it will read them all into an I16 array. When the operation is done, the binary file reference is closed, and the program goes back to the **Initialize** state:

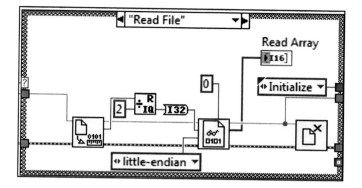

5. When the user clicks on the **Exit** button, the **"End"** state is entered, where the stop condition of the state machine is set to true:

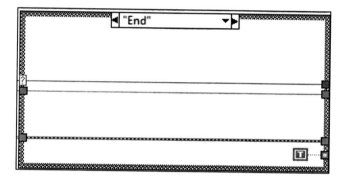

How it works...

This program allows a user to read or write an I16 array from/to a file. It opens or creates a binary file called test. When the user clicks on write, the program writes the I16 array into the binary file. When the user clicks on read, it reads the I16 array from the file. To read the file, the program must know exactly what is in there and how it is formatted.

Working with TDMS files

Technical Data Management Stream (**TDMS**) is a LabVIEW file type for data storage. It has its own format with three levels of structure: root, group, and channel. Each file can contain an unlimited number of groups, and each group can contain an unlimited number of channels.

A TDMS file is in binary format, so it is smaller compared to ASCII. It organizes the data in three groups, so that there is no need to create a custom structure. TDMS is selected when the file size needs to be smaller than an ASCII file.

How to do it...

Create the state machine using following steps:

1. The first state is **Initialize**. It opens or creates the `test.tdms` file in the same folder as the calling VI and transits to the next state.

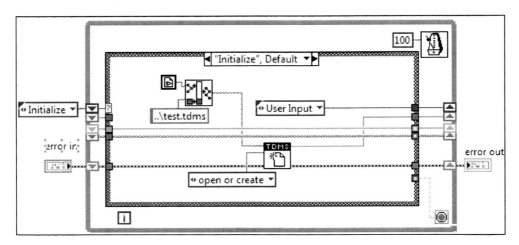

2. The next state is **"User Input"**. It waits for the user to click on the **Read**, **Write**, or **Exit** button and transits to the corresponding state:

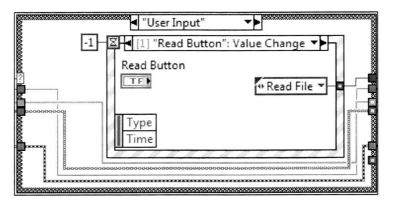

3. When the write button is clicked on, the program transits into the **"Generate Data"** state. In this state, it generates 500 random numbers and marks them as **Pass** if a number is greater than 0.5; else it is marked as **False**. After the data is generated, it is passed to the next state. The program transits to the **Write File** state.

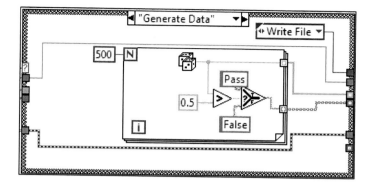

4. After the data is generated, the next state is the **"Write File"** state. It writes the random number in the **Data** channel under the **Measurement** group, and it writes the test result in the **P/F** channel under the **Result** group:

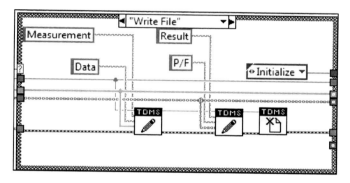

5. If a user clicks on the read file button, the program transits into the **"Read File"** state. In this state, it reads data from the **Data** channel and results from the **P/F** channel under the **Measurement** and **Result** groups respectively. After reading the data, the reference to the TDMS file is closed and the program transits back to the **User Input** state:

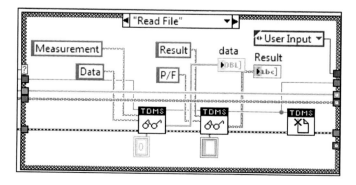

6. If a user clicks on the exit button, the program transits into the **"End"** state, where the state machine stop condition is set to true:

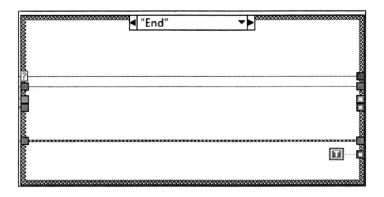

How it works...

This program allows a user to read and write to a TDMS file. When a user clicks on the write button, it writes an array of double precision numbers and the corresponding test results into a TDMS file. If the read button is clicked on, the program reads the array and result, and displays both on the front panel. The data and result are stored in the **Data** and **P/F** channels under **Measurement** and **Result** groups respectively.

Using Telnet and FTP with files

Telnet allows users to log in to another machine to perform file operations. **File Transfer Protocol** (**FTP**) allows file transfer from one machine to another. In this example, we will demonstrate how to use telnet to log in to a Unix machine and create a folder. With the folder created, FTP is used for transferring a file to that folder.

How to do it...

We will create a state machine to use telnet and ftp for transferring files using the following steps:

1. Create the state machine, as shown in the following screenshot. The first state is **"User input"**. It waits for the user to click on start and populate a cluster with values from the front panel controls.

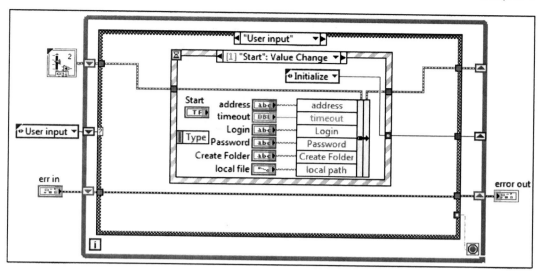

2. The next state is **"Initialize"**. It creates a telnet session with user input IP address of the Unix machine:

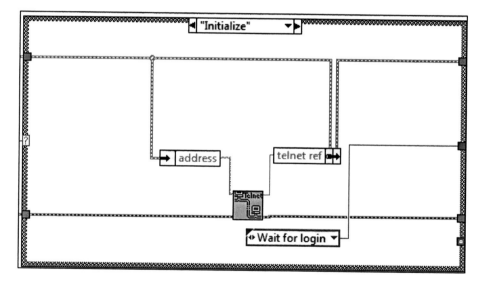

3. The next state is **"Wait for login"**. The state waits for the string **login:** to appear. If it does, the program transits to the **Send Login** state. If not, after the user-specified timeout has expired, the program transits to the **Time out** state. See the following screenshot for reference:

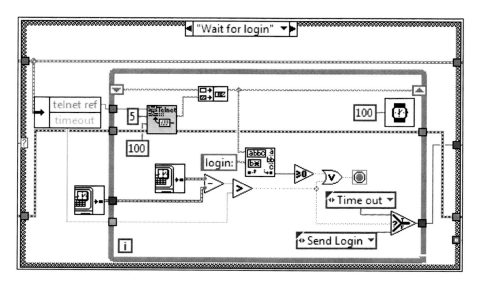

4. After the string **login:** appears, the **"Send Login"** state sends the user-specified login credential to the telnet session:

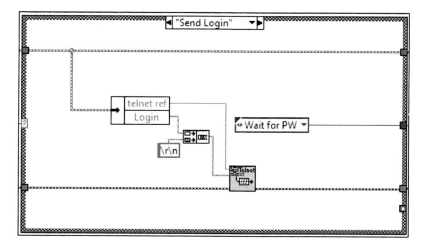

5. The next state is **"Wait for PW"**. The state waits for the string **Password:** to appear. If it does, the program transits to the **Send PW** state. If not, after the user-specified timeout has expired, the program transits to the **Time out** state as shown in the following screenshot:

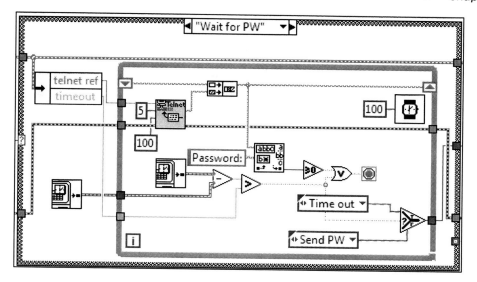

6. After the string **Password** appears, the program transits to the **"Send PW"** state. In this state, the user-specified password is sent to the telnet session:

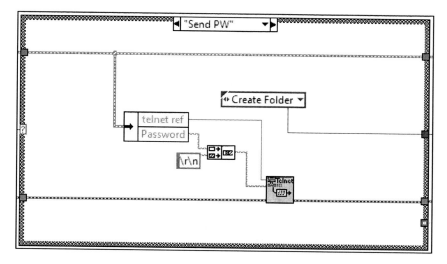

7. After logging in, the program arrives at the **"Create Folder"** state, which sends the `mkdir` command with the user-specified folder name to the telnet session to create a folder. See the following screenshot for reference:

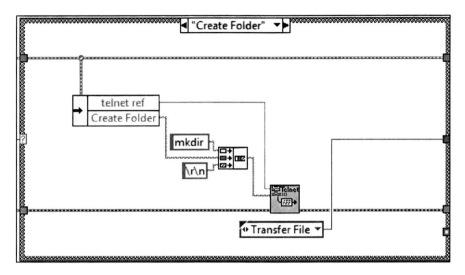

8. The next state is **"Transfer File"**. After the folder is created with a telnet session, FTP is used to to transfer a file to the folder:

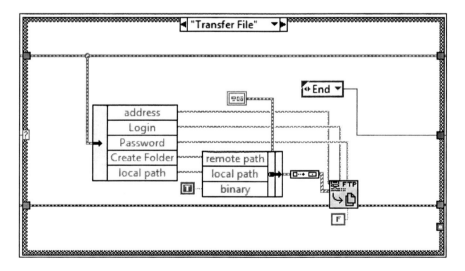

9. The **"Time out"** state is only entered if there is a time out condition for the telnet session. A dialog box will appear to alert the user of the event. See the following screenshot for reference:

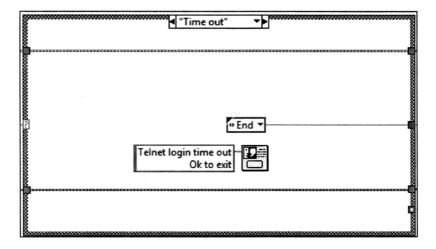

10. Finally, the program enters the **"End"** state, where the telnet session is closed if it exists:

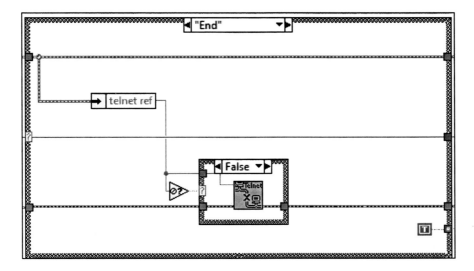

How it works...

This program waits for the user to specify the IP address, username, password, and so on. With the user input, a telnet session is created with a Unix machine. During the session, a folder is created. After the folder is created, a file is transferred to the folder through FTP.

Working with a database

A database is a common method to store a huge amount of data. It can group data into different tables and relate the tables through keys. To retrieve data from a database, a query can be used, which will make access to the data quick and easy. In this example, we will demonstrate how to work with a database in LabVIEW.

How to do it...

We will implement functions for a database in an action engine, using the following steps:

1. Create a **Universal Data Link** (**UDL**) file. The file contains database connection information. It is used when the database is initialized in the program. Create a file and change its extension to udl. Configure the file based on the setting of the type of database being accessed. The configuration detail is beyond the scope of this book.

2. Create the action engine, as shown in the following screenshot. To use the action engine, the **"Initialize"** command must first be used to establish a database session based on the specified **UDL Path**. The reference of the UDL file and the table name of the table are stored in shift registers.

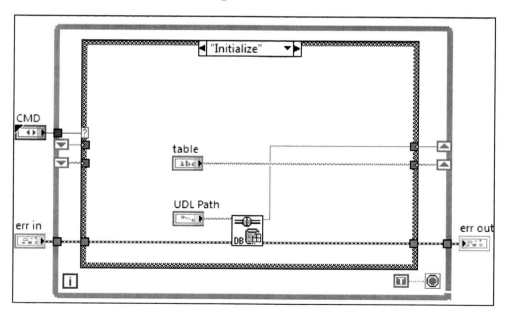

3. The **"Insert Row"** command allows a user to insert data into the database. See the following screenshot for reference:

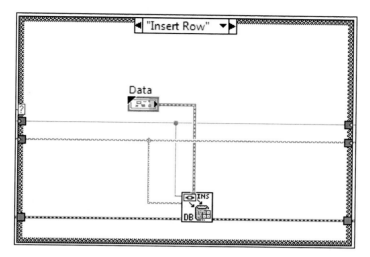

4. The **"Query Row"** command allows the user to search the database for a person's information with a given full name.

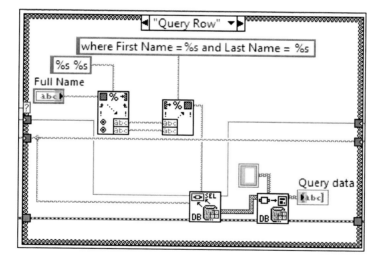

5. The **"Close Ref"** command closes the database session to free up resources:

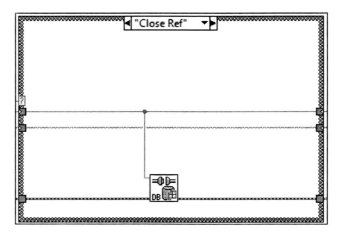

How it works...

This example creates an action engine that works with a database. For the action engine to run correctly, the Initialize command must first be executed to establish a database session. After that, the user can add data and query data from the database.

8
Understanding Data Acquisition

In this chapter, we will cover:

- ▶ Using MAX
- ▶ Working with VISA
- ▶ Using VISA servers
- ▶ Controlling an oscilloscope
- ▶ Using a simple DAQ device
- ▶ Using a CompactDAQ

Introduction

This chapter presents examples of doing data acquisition in LabVIEW. We will show how to use LabVIEW to communicate with different instruments, such as an oscilloscope, an USB DAQ, and a CompactDAQ. We will also explore MAX, VISA, and VISA server to see how they enhance the communication between LabVIEW and an instrument.

Using MAX

Measurement and Automation Explorer (MAX) is a software used along with LabVIEW for instrument management. In this recipe, we will demonstrate how to send hex number to instrument, create a DAQMX task, and create a simulated instrument within MAX. A simulated instrument can be used when we try to program an instrument, but we do not have the instrument at hand.

How to do it...

We will start by using MAX to send hex number to an instrument. This is only applicable for instruments that support hex number communication.

1. To send hex values to an instrument, plug in a serial instrument that communicates with hex number and open MAX. Click on **Open VISA Test Panel** to start communicating with the instrument. See the following screenshot to see where the instrument will show up in MAX and the location of **Open VISA Test Panel**:

2. In **VISA Test Panel**, you can enter bytes of hex values, separated by \, and click on **Write** to send it to the instrument. After the values are written, the actual values written to the instrument and its status is displayed.

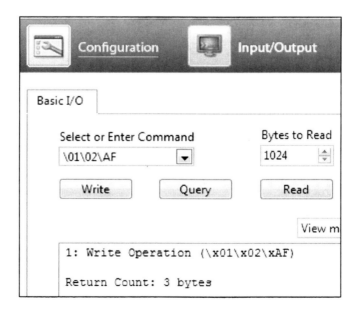

3. On top of the **VISA Test Panel**, there is an option for **NI I/O Trace**, which is a tool to trace the communication between the host PC and the instrument. The following screenshot shows that a write action is being performed:

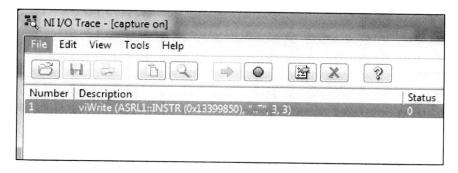

4. Another useful thing to do in MAX is to add a simulated instrument to a PC. Right-click on **Devices and Interfaces** and select **Create New....** as shown in the following screenshot:

5. Double-click on **Simulated NI-DAQmx Device or Modular Instrument**, as shown in the following screenshot:

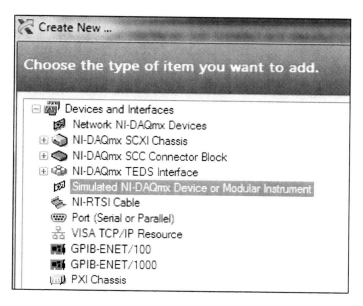

6. For our example, select **NI cDAQ-9191**:

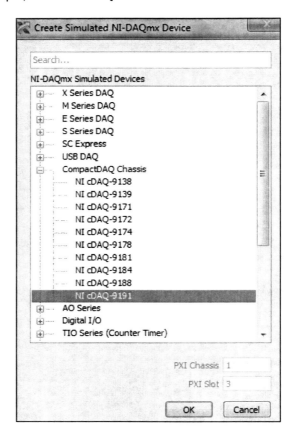

7. Click on **Configure Simulated cDAQ Chassis...** and add the module **NI 9201** to it. See the following screenshot. After we have added and configured the simulated device, we can use it in MAX and LabVIEW, even though the instrument is not actually connected.

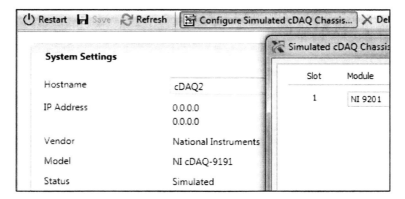

8. Another useful thing that can be done in MAX is configuring a DAQ task. Right-click on the simulated instrument that we just created, and click on **Create Task…**.

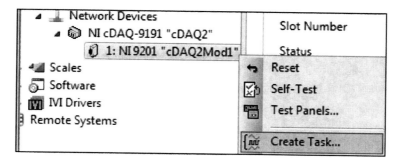

9. Select **Voltage** under **Analog Input**, as shown in the following screenshot:

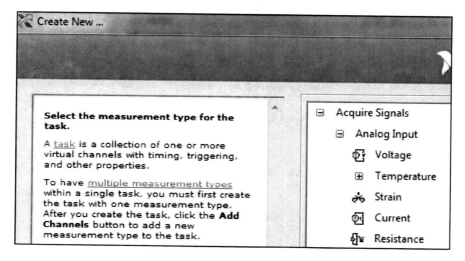

10. Select channel 0, **ai0**.

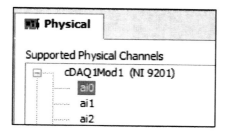

11. Now, the physical channel can be configured as needed.

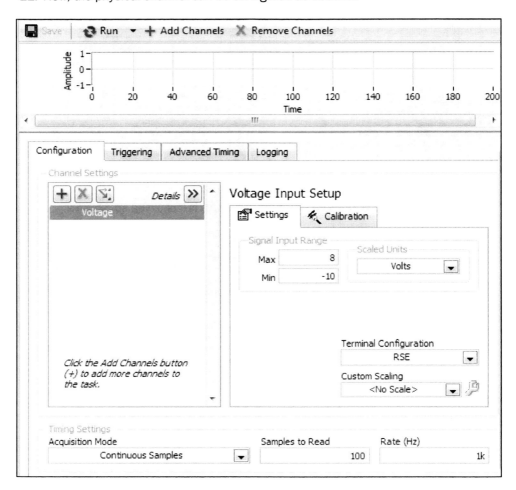

12. After the task is created, the task shows up in MAX under **Data Neighborhood**.

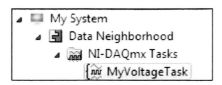

13. The task will also show up when you put a task constant in a block diagram. See the following screenshot for a simple way to start a task, to get samples from the channel of the task, and to stop the task.

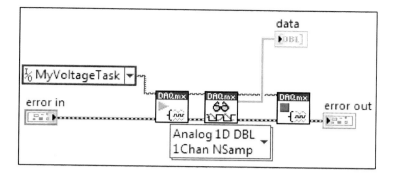

How it works...

In this recipe, we covered three useful tasks that we can do in MAX: send hex values to an instrument, create a simulated instrument, and create a task.

Sending hex values to an instrument is very valuable, since many older instruments still use protocol that send and receive hex values. For NI VISA version newer than 5.1, each byte of the hex value is preceded with \. For versions older than 5.1, each byte of the hex value is preceded with **\x**.

Creating a simulated instrument is very useful when we want to try it out in a simulated environment before actually making the purchase. This can potentially save a lot of development time, since we don't have to wait for the instrument to arrive before we start programming. We can create a simulated instrument and start programming with it immediately.

Creating a task allows us to set up a physical channel with ranges, sampling rate, and so on. This way we don't have to set up the instrument in our LabVIEW program and programming complexity is decreased. However, the task becomes another accessory that we need to transfer when we move the program from one PC to another. Keep in mind that for some instruments, creating a task is the only way to configure a channel.

Working with VISA

The **Virtual Instrument Software Architecture** (**VISA**) is a one stop for instrument automation. VISA can be used to control any instruments that use Serial, GPIB, Ethernet, PXI, VXI, and USB. VISA is already built-in for LabVIEW. In this recipe, we will create an action engine with VISA functions.

How to do it...

We will start by creating an action engine that can be used to read and write through VISA.

1. Create the action engine, as shown in the following screenshot. The first function is **"Initialize"**. It creates a VISA session based on the VISA resource name, and saves the reference to a shift register.

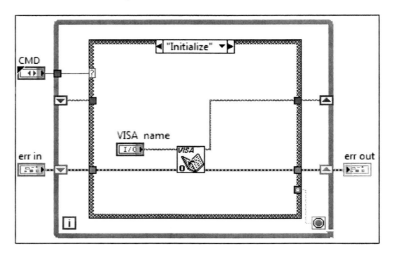

2. The next function is **"Read"**. It reads the specified number of bytes from the buffer.

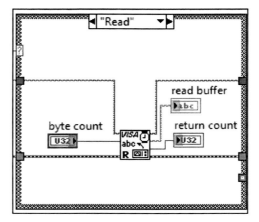

3. The next function is **"Write"**. It writes the input string to the buffer.

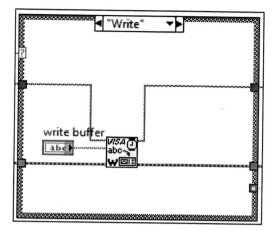

4. The last function is **"End"**. It closes the VISA session.

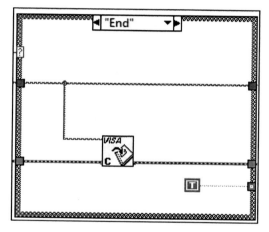

How it works...

The **Initialize** function must be used first. After the function is used, a VISA session is created and its reference is saved in a shift register. Subsequently, the **Read, Write**, and **End** functions will use the saved session reference to perform their functions.

Using VISA servers

VISA servers allow a server and client relationship among PC on the same network. The relationship will allow the PCs to control each other instrumentation. This recipe will demonstrate how to set up and use VISA servers.

How to do it...

We will start by configuring the VISA server.

1. On the server computer that is actually connected with an instrument, open MAX. Navigate to **Tools** | **NI-VISA** | **VISA Options**.

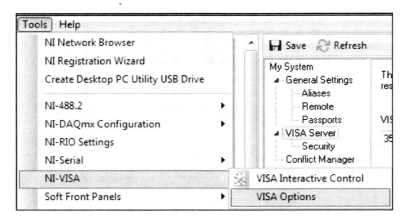

2. Under **Security**, put the IP address of the PC that is allowed to access the server. In the example, ***** is used, which means that there is no access restriction.

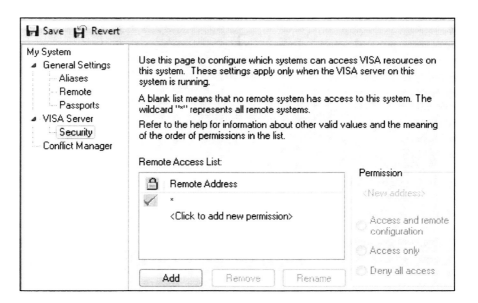

3. After the server is set up, the server PC and its instruments will be shown up under **Remote Systems** in MAX of the client PC. The IP address of the server PC is crossed out in this example for privacy reasons.

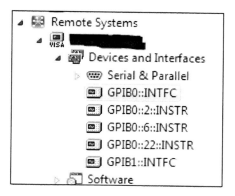

How it works...

In this example, we set up the VISA server on the server PC to share all of its instruments with every PC on the same network. For security reasons, instead of granting universal access, specific IP addresses can be entered to restrict access to certain PCs on network. Once the VISA server is set up on the server machine, any client machine can address the instruments connected to the server machine directly. People may say that we can use remote desktop to connect to the server machine and use its instruments. However, to do this, we must have the LabVIEW development environment installed on that server.

Controlling an oscilloscope

Controlling an instrument is a common task when writing a LabVIEW program. In this recipe, we will demonstrate how to control a TDS3012 oscilloscope. For other instruments, try to search for the corresponding driver. If a driver is not available, navigate to **Tool | Instrumentation | Create Instrument Driver Project** to code the driver based on a NI provided template.

How to do it...

To start creating an application to control the instrument, we will search and download the applicable driver. The driver is written by people who are experienced with the instrument, but keep in mind that there is no guarantee that it will work.

1. First, download the driver of our oscilloscope. Select **Help and Find Instrument Driver**. The **Configure Search** dialog will appear, as shown in the following screenshot. Now we perform a search. Click on **Login** to log into your NI account. If you do not have an account already, you can get an account for free at www.ni.com. If the instrument is connected to the PC, click on **Scan for Instruments**. If the instrument is not connected, search with the criteria given.

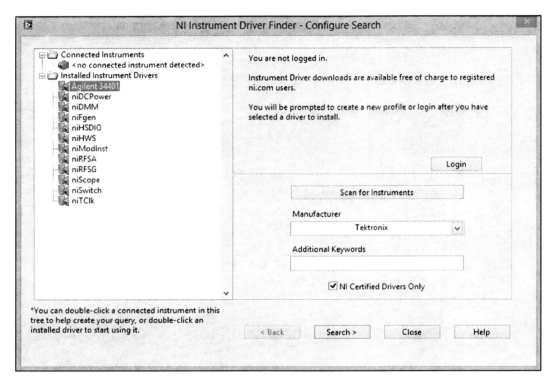

2. The following screenshot shows the results of our search. Double-click on the driver and follow the installation instructions. After installing and restarting LabVIEW, the new driver is located in the **Instrument I/O | Instr Drivers** palette.

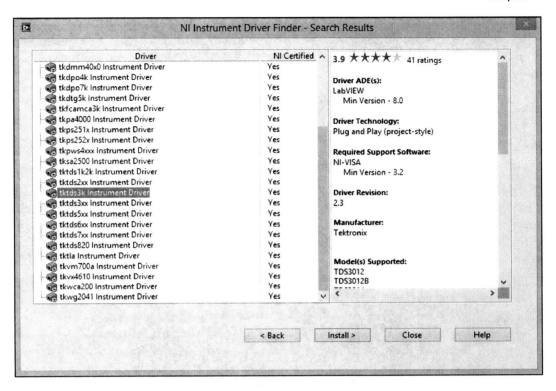

3. Build the state machine, as shown in the following screenshot. It goes to the **"User Input"** state to populate all user inputs to the input cluster when the **Start** button is clicked on and transits to the **Initialize** state.

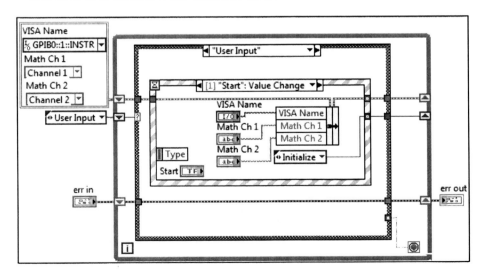

4. When the **Exit** button is clicked on, the program transits to the **End** state.

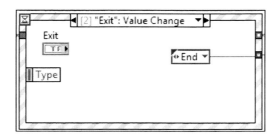

5. When the **Start** button is clicked on, the program transits to the **"Initialize"** state. In the state, it initializes the TDS3012 oscilloscope.

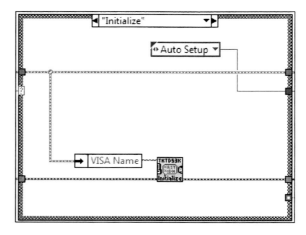

6. The next state is **"Auto Setup"**, where the auto set command is issued to TDS3012.

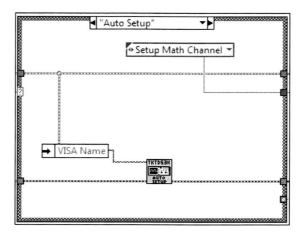

7. The next state is **"Setup Math Channel"**, which enables the math channel and specifies which two channels will be used for the math operation.

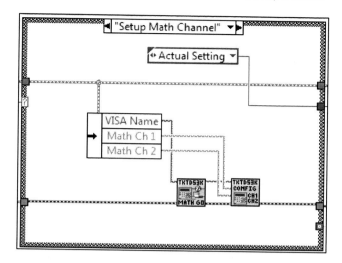

8. The next state, **"Actual Setting"**, reads the record length, sampling mode, and sampling rate of the instrument and outputs them to the screen.

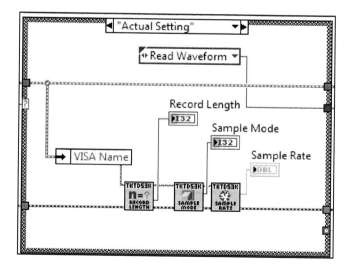

9. The next state reads the waveform from channel 1 and outputs it to a waveform chart indicator.

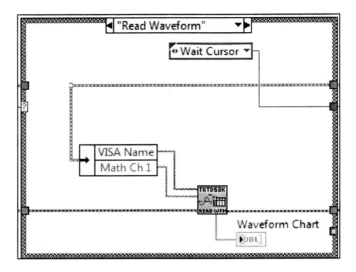

10. The next state is **"Wait Cursor"**. A dialog will appear to pause the program until the user adjusts cursors on the physical oscilloscope and clicks on **OK** on the software user interface.

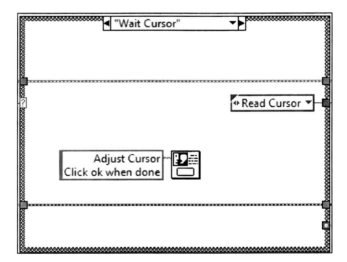

11. The next state is **"Read Cursor"**. After the user finishes adjusting the cursors, this state reads the delta of the cursors on the x axis. The program goes back to the **User Input** state to wait for the input.

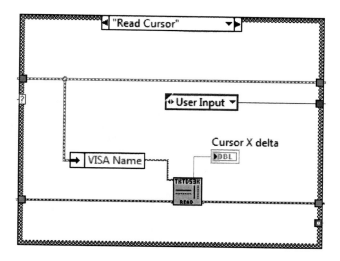

12. If the user clicks on the **Exit** button, the program goes to the **"End"** state. The state closes the VISA session and sets the stop condition of the state machine to `true`.

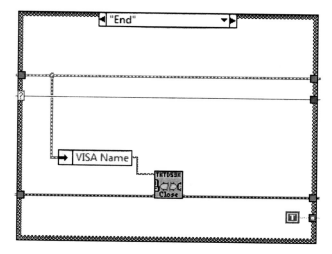

13. The following screenshot shows the front panel of the program.

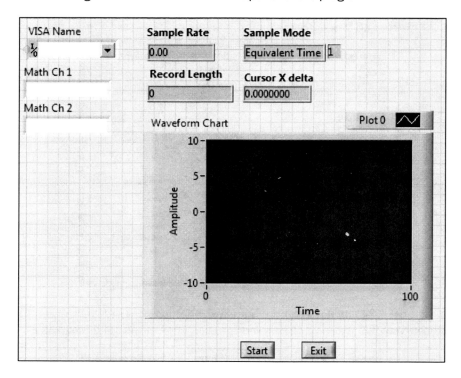

How it works...

This program controls a TDS3012 oscilloscope. It waits for the user input to set up the oscilloscope. When the user enters the input and clicks on **Start**, the program sets up the oscilloscope and captures the waveform. With the waveform, the program displays a dialog and waits for the user to adjust the x axis cursors of the oscilloscope. Once everything is done, the delta of the cursors is displayed.

Using a simple DAQ device

Buying a DAQ device does not have to be costly. The NI USB-6000 is a USB-based DAQ device with 8 SE/4 DIFF analog input with 10 kS/s sampling rate and 12 bits resolution. It also has 4 DIO and a 32 bits counter. With so many features, it only costs $149. In this recipe, we will use DAQmx to work with such a device.

How to do it...

We will write an application that controls a NI USB-6000 with a state machine.

1. Build the state machine, as shown in the following screenshot. The first state is **"User Input"**. When a user clicks on the **Start** button, it puts all user inputs onto a cluster and sends it to the next state.

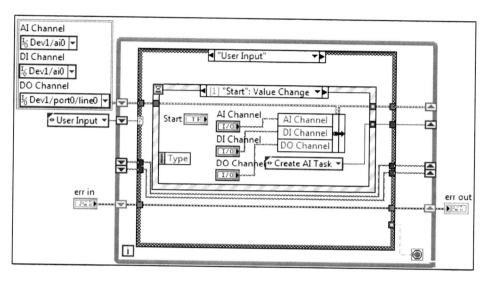

2. The next state is **"Create AI Task"**. It sets up an analog input channel for data acquisition.

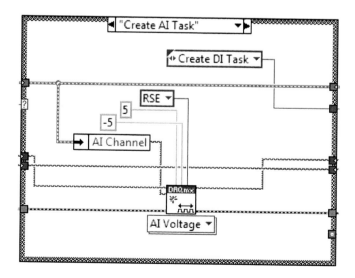

3. The next state is **"Create DI Task"**. It sets up a digital input channel for data acquisition.

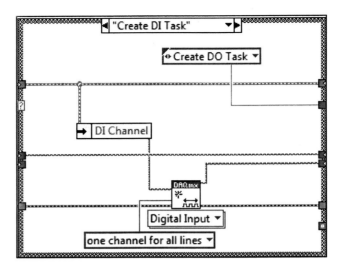

4. The next task is **"Create DO Task"**. It sets up a digital output channel for outputting a digital signal.

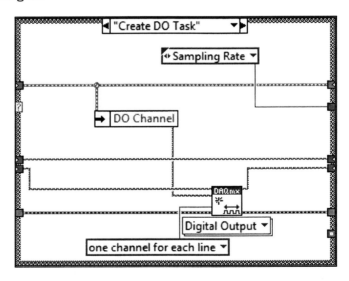

5. The next state is **"Sampling Rate"**. It defines the sampling rate for both the analog task and the digital task.

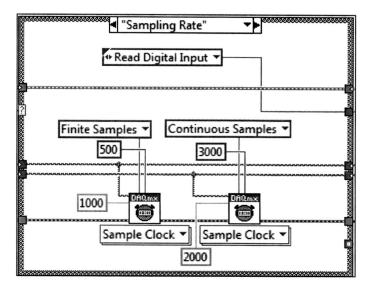

6. The next state is **"Read Digital Input"**. The state machine will continue to go back to this state until the 0th and 1st bit of the digital input goes high. In this case, when the 0th and 1st bit go high, the state machine will go to the next state.

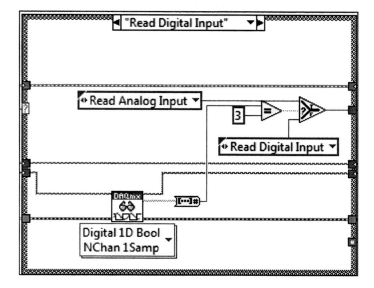

7. The next state is **"Read Analog Input"**. It reads one sample from the analog channel and outputs it to a chart.

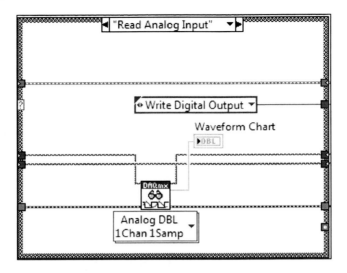

8. The next state is **"Write Digital Output"**. It sets the specified digital line to true.

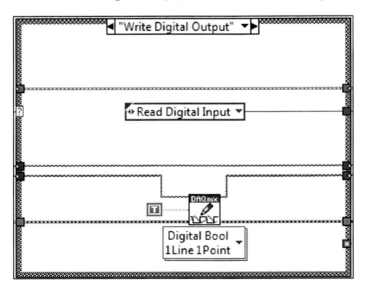

9. When the user clicks on **Exit**, both the analog and digital tasks are cleared, and the stop condition of the state machine is set to true.

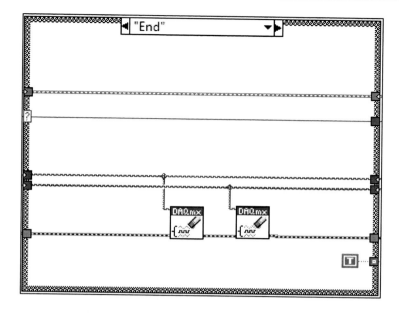

10. The front panel of the program is shown in the following screenshot. It consists of **AI Channel**, **DI Channel**, and **DO Channel**, which are analog and digital channels used on the device. The chart displays the analog data acquired. The **Start** button is for starting the program, and the **Exit** button is for terminating the program.

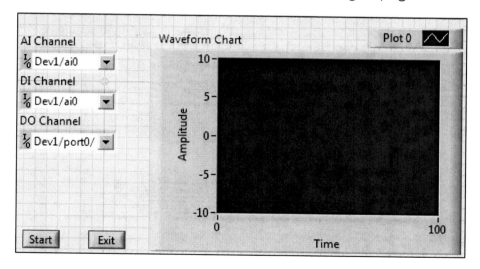

How it works...

This program sets up a very simple and inexpensive DAQ device. It sets up the device to wait for a digital input and reads an analog input when the correct digital input is detected. After the analog input acquisition is done, it sets the digital output to high to signal that the acquisition is done.

Using a CompactDAQ

Relative to the NI USB-6000, the CompactDAQ is more complex and more expensive. However, it allows users to buy different kinds of signal conditioning modules for different data acquisition needs. In this recipe, we will demonstrate how to use a cDAQ-9138 with a NI 9211 thermal couple module and a NI 9234 acceleration module.

How to do it...

After working with a NI USB-6000, we will write a program that controls a CompactDAQ with a thermal couple module and an acceleration module. Even though the instruments are different, programming a USB-6000 and a CompactDAQ is very similar.

1. Build the state machine, as shown in the following screenshot. The first state is **"User Input"**. When the user clicks on **Start**, it populates the input cluster with user inputs and sends the cluster to the next state.

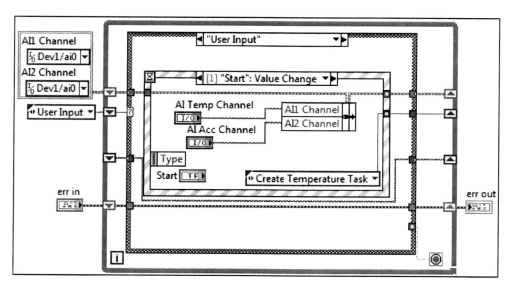

2. If the user clicks on **Exit**, the exit event case is fired, and the state machine goes to the **End** state.

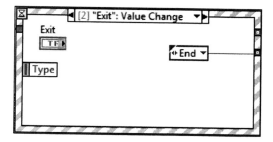

3. The next state is **"Create Temperature Task"**. It sets up an analog input channel on the thermal couple module for temperature data acquisition.

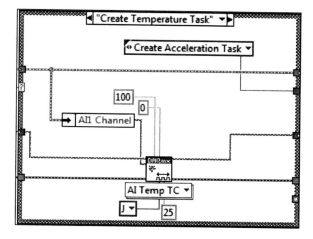

4. The next state is **"Create Acceleration Task"**. It sets up an analog input signal on the acceleration module for data acquisition.

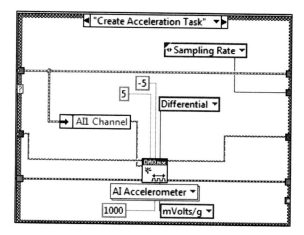

5. The next state is **"Sampling Rate"**. It sets up the sampling rate for the analog task with both the channels.

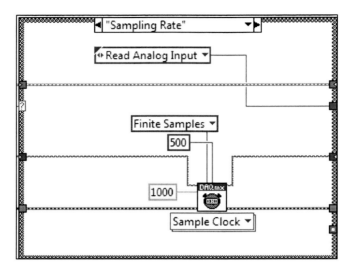

6. The next state is **"Read Analog Input"**. It reads both the temperature and acceleration into a 1-D array. When this is done, the state machine goes back to the **User Input** state to wait for the user input.

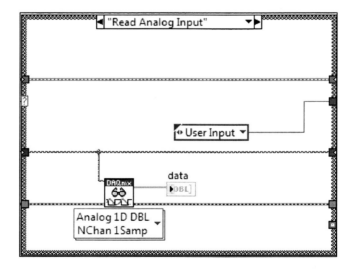

7. When the user clicks on **Exit**, the program enters the **"End"** state. It clears the task and sets the stop condition of the state machine to true.

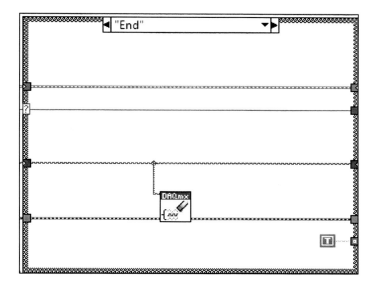

8. The front panel of the program is shown in the following screenshot. It consists of **AI Temp Channel** and **AI Acc Channel**, which are the selected channels for the temperature and acceleration module. The two elements in the **data** array are temperature and acceleration acquired from the modules. The **Start** and **Exit** buttons are to start and terminate the program.

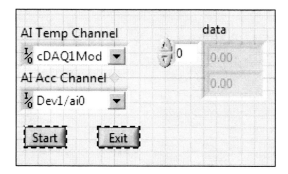

How it works...

This program uses a cDAQ-9138 with a NI 9211 thermal couple module and a NI 9234 acceleration module. It waits for the user input and sets up the modules to capture temperature and acceleration data on demand.

9
Simplifying Code

In this chapter, we will cover:

- ▸ Using polymorphic VI
- ▸ Simplifying logic selection
- ▸ Using an array for computation
- ▸ Formatting into string
- ▸ Speedy array search
- ▸ Using relative paths in EXE

Introduction

Many people start programming in LabVIEW without knowing how to keep their code simple and neat. At the end, they end up walking up a very steep slope or giving up altogether. This chapter presents tips on simplifying LabVIEW code that will make programing in LabVIEW easy and fun.

Using polymorphic VI

Polymorphic VI is a VI that can exist in different forms. It allows the grouping of multiple VIs into one VI that can take different forms. In this recipe, we will demonstrate how to build a polymorphic VI that can handle math operations, such as addition, subtraction, multiplication, division, combination, and permutation.

How to do it...

1. Create a VI for the add function.

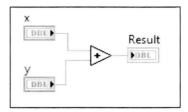

2. Create a VI for the subtract function.

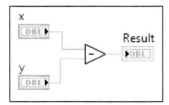

3. Create a VI for the multiply function.

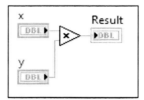

4. Create a VI for the division function. It calculates the result of the division in floating point. It also calculate the quotient and remainder separately.

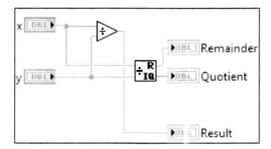

5. Create a VI for the combination function.

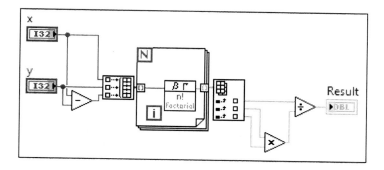

6. Create a VI for the permutation function.

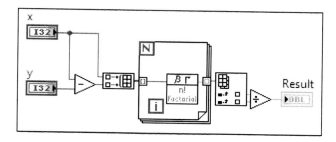

7. The VI for each function must have the same input and output connected in the icon terminals. After a VI is created for each function, create a polymorphic VI. This VI will group all the previous VIs together. See the following screenshot:

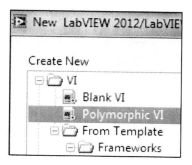

8. Add all the function VIs into the polymorphic VI, as shown in the following screenshot:

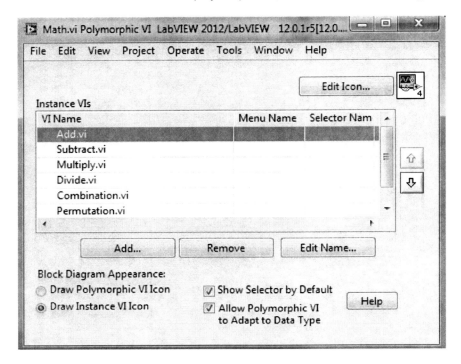

9. Create an example VI that uses the polymorphic VI. It has a while loop with an event structure. Within the **Calculate** event case, there is a case structure consists of one case per function. When the mode is selected and the **Calculate** button is clicked on, the program will select the corresponding function and output the result.

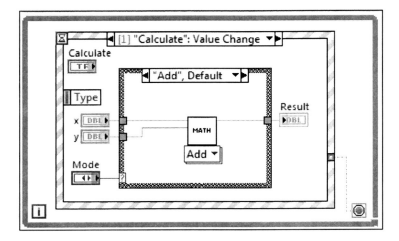

10. Another event case is **Panel Close?**. When a user closes the program, it will stop the program by setting the stop condition to `true` and not discard the close panel event, so that the panel will close.

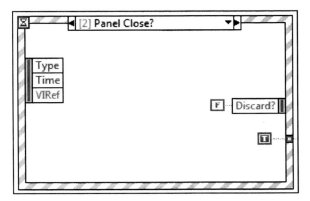

How it works...

In this example, we implemented a polymorphic VI that can add, subtract, multiply, divide, and calculate combination and permutation with inputs x and y. To avoid confusion, the connector pane terminals for each function VI should be arranged in the same way.

In the example VI that uses the polymorphic VI, it waits for the user to select the function, enter inputs, and click on **Calculate**. Inside the **Calculate** event case, another case structure resides and contains the corresponding instance of the polymorphic VI in each case. The correct case is selected based on the user input. This is a great way to clean up code, but most importantly, to re-use code.

Simplifying logic selection

Many text-based programmers find the case structure in LabVIEW very hard to read, especially when the case structure is nested with multiple layers. In this recipe, we will examine a multiple-layers case structure and how to convert the multiple layers into one.

How to do it...

We will demonstrate how a nested case structure can be a concern by building a simple program with a four-layers nested case structure.

1. Build the block diagram as shown in the following screenshot. It is a case structure with four layers. The true case of each layer will give us access to the case structure of the next layer. The output string is **TRUE** if ABCD = TTTT, TTFT, or TTFF. Otherwise, the output string is **FALSE**.

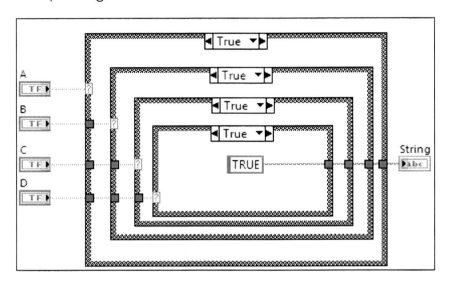

2. The output of the third layer is a **FALSE** string constant.

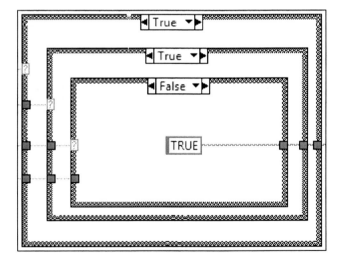

3. To convert the four-layers nested case structure into a single case structure, see the following screenshot. All Boolean inputs are built into an array, and the array is converted into a decimal number with the top Boolean being the least significant bit. In the following case, it shows the conditions when a **TRUE** string constant is the output. The Boolean controls are built into an array with the `Build Array` node, and the array is converted into an unsigned long (U32) number with the `Boolean Array To Number` node. The order of the bits are DCBA. If the binary number is 0001, A is true. If the binary number is 1000, D is true. If the binary number is 11, it is equivalent to 0011.

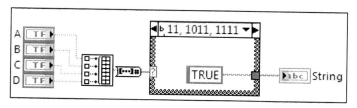

4. To make the decimal number converted from the Boolean array more clear, we can convert the radix of the case structure into binary. Right click on the case structure and select the **Binary** option.

5. For all other conditions, the constant string output is **FALSE**.

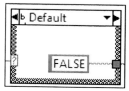

How it works...

In this recipe, we simplify a four-layers case structure into a single case structure. To do this, we combine all the Boolean inputs into an array, convert the array into a number, and use the number as an input for the single case structure. To clarify it, we convert the display value of the case structure into binary, so that the value for each case structure is explicit for each Boolean.

Using an array for computation

If the same mathematical operation is needed for a set of numbers, performing the operation in an array is very efficient. However, if the operation is needed only for a subset of the numbers that meet certain criteria, looping is still required. In this recipe, we will demonstrate how to iterate through each element of an array and how to perform a mathematical operation on an array.

How to do it...

We will start by creating a sinusoidal wave one element at a time, and add one to the data point that is equal to the amplitude.

1. Create the block diagram, as shown in the following screenshot. With the amplitude input, a sinusoidal array of one element is generated. If the element is equal to the amplitude, the element increments by 1 and outputs to a waveform chart. If not, the element is outputted to the waveform directly.

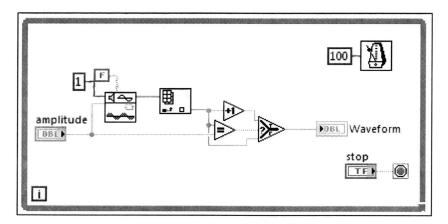

2. The front panel in the following screenshot shows that at the positive peaks of the sinusoidal wave, there are additional spikes:

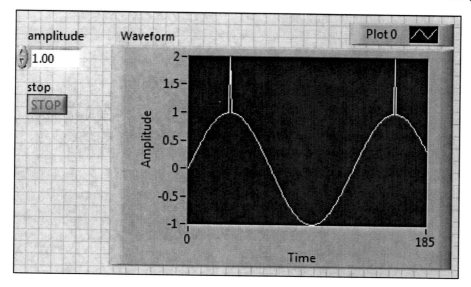

3. The next example with input amplitude builds three waveforms: triangular, square, and sinusoidal with 50 samples, each with a sampling rate of 1,000 samples per second. The three waveforms are built into an array and all the elements are multiplied by 2 and added to 6.

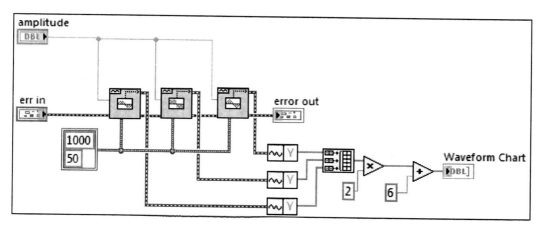

4. The front panel, in the following screenshot, shows the resulting waveform:

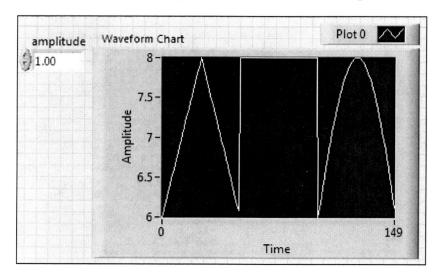

How it works...

In this recipe, we demonstrated how to iterate through an array and process the elements based on criteria. For situations where a set of numbers need to be processed with the same operation, building the numbers into an array and processing the array as a whole is more efficient. In this case, there is no need to iterate through each element.

Formatting into string

To create a string with substrings converted from values of different data types, the values of different types are converted into strings and concatenated. Another way is to use the `Format Into String` node. In this recipe, we will demonstrate both methods.

How to do it...

We will start by combining multiple strings into one string with the Concatenate Strings.

1. The following block diagram converts different number types and enum into strings and concatenates them together using the `Concatenate Strings` node.

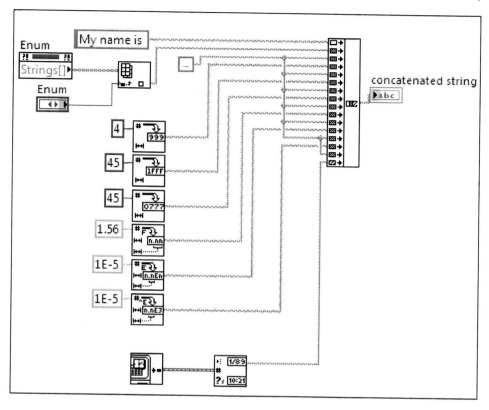

2. The front panel is shown in the following screenshot. It consists of the input **Enum** and the output **concatenated string**.

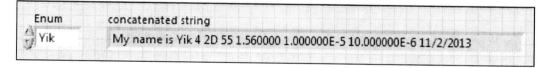

3. To perform the same task with the `Format Into String` node, see the following screenshot. We specify all conversions with the format string input of the `Format Into String` node. The input string **My name is** is wired to the initial string input. It will appear at the beginning of the resulting string. The **Enum** input corresponds to the **%s** argument of the format string input, and the enum will get converted into a string. Similarly, **%d** is used for decimal, **%x** for hexadecimal, **%o** for octal, **%f** for floating point, **%e** for exponential notation, **%^e** for engineering, and **%<%m/%d/%y>T** for month/date/year.

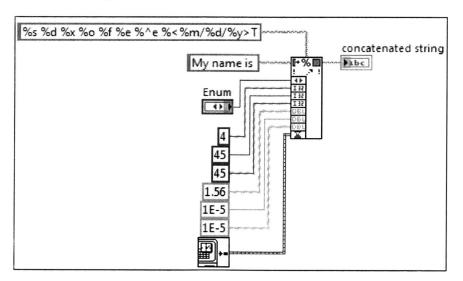

How it works...

In this recipe, we demonstrated how to use the `Concatenate Strings` node and the `Format Into String` node. For simple strings, the `Concatenate Strings` node is used. For more complex strings, the Format Into String node is used. For Format Into String, note that enum, timestamp, and different number types do not need to be converted separately. Also, to include a constant string to the resulting string, the constant string can be added into the format string input directly.

Speedy array search

Array search is a common task in programming. In this recipe, we will demonstrate three ways of searching for an element in an array and extract the element from another array with the same location index.

How to do it...

We will start searching an array by using a loop.

1. The following front panel applies to all examples. **Array** is the array that we are searching with the **Person** parameter. The 1D array contains values corresponding to **Array**.

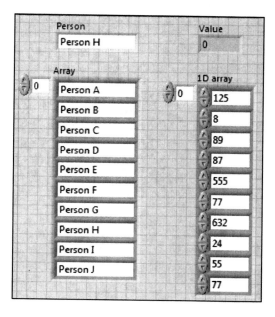

2. The first way is a simple loop search. It is the most straightforward, but also the slowest. It loops through each element of the search array, and when the search element is found, the index is used to extract the element from another array.

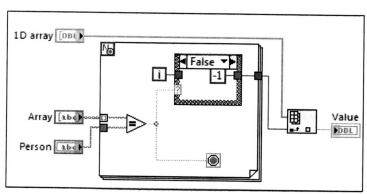

3. The next method is using the Search 1D Array function built into LabVIEW. This is a linear search similar to the loop approach, so there is not much performance improvement, but it makes the code a lot more elegant.

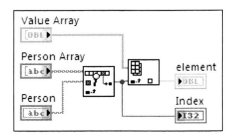

4. The last method is the variant method. First, create a dummy variant value. With a while loop, we will create attributes for the dummy variant. The name of each attributes correspond to each element of **Person Array**. The value of each attributes correspond to each element of **Value Array**. By doing this, a relationship is built between the elements of **Person Array** and **Value Array**. When this is a setup, the variant is used for searching.

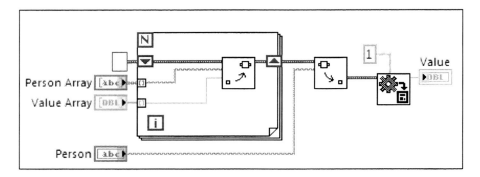

How it works...

In this recipe, we demonstrated three ways of searching an array. We can iterate through an array one element at a time. We can use the Search 1D Array function in LabVIEW. We can also use the attributes in a variant, which is a lot faster.

Using relative paths in EXE

Path information is used to access files in software. Some programmer would hardcode the path information directly into the software, which makes maintaining the software troublesome. In this recipe, we will demonstrate how to use relative path to access files stored in a relative location of the main VI or EXE.

How to do it...

We will start by creating a text file that the EXE will access.

1. Create the text file and save it in the same folder as the caller VI or the EXE. See the following screenshot:

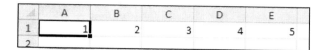

2. Create the VI, as shown in the following screenshot. It has a while loop with an event structure. When the **Read File** button is clicked on, it creates the path of the text file, reads the text file, and outputs the content of the file into an array.

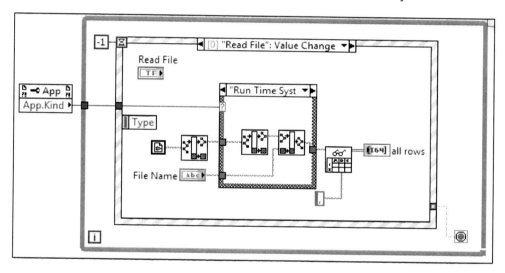

3. The path is different depending on the code being run is in the development mode or in an EXE. See the following screenshot for how the path is modified when the code is run in the development mode.

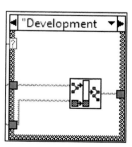

4. When the **Exit** button is clicked on, the stop condition of the while loop is set to true, and the program stops.

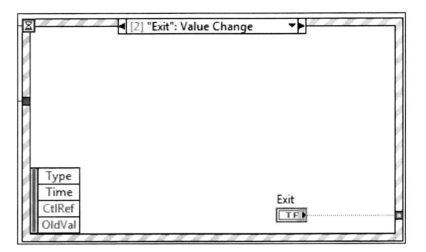

How it works...

This recipe demonstrated how to read a file relative to the calling VI or EXE. In this example, the current VI path constant is used. In the development mode, the current VI path is the location where we save the VI. For EXE, the main VI is embedded into the EXE, so there is an extra level to the path. The program must determine what mode it is running in and choose how to process the current VI path information correctly.

10

Working with External Code and Applications

In this chapter, we will cover:

- ► Compiling a DLL
- ► Using a .NET DLL
- ► Debugging a .NET DLL
- ► Using C-based DLL
- ► Using ActiveX
- ► Building a web service
- ► Using SMTP to send e-mail

Introduction

This chapter presents examples on how to work with external codes and applications within LabVIEW. Within LabVIEW, we will compile a DLL and work with different kinds of DLLs, that are .NET and C-based. We will also work with ActiveX, web service, and SMTP.

Compiling a DLL

Dynamic Link Library (**DLL**) contains executable functions that can be accessed by other programs in different platform. In this recipe, we will demonstrate how to compile a DLL in LabVIEW.

How to do it...

We will create a DLL within LabVIEW. First, we will create a project.

1. Create a project with a factorial function, a square function, and an example that calls the functions from a DLL after the functions are compiled into one.

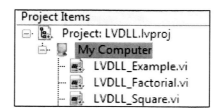

2. After we have created the project, we will create the square function. Create the block diagram as shown in the following screenshot for the square function. It squares the input and outputs the result.

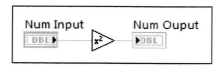

3. On the front panel, connect the input and output to the icon terminals.

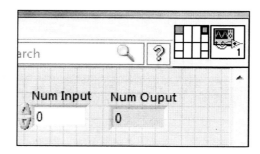

4. After we have created the square function, we will create the factorial function. Create the following block diagram for the factorial function. At the top, it uses the built-in factorial function in LabVIEW to calculate factorial. At the bottom, it calculates the factorial with iteration. The default case is for any **Num Input** that is not less than or equal to 1.

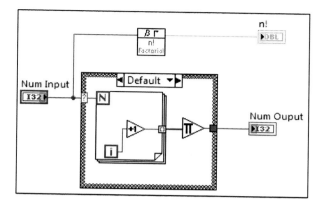

5. For **Num Input** values less than or equal to 1, the output from the case structure is 1.

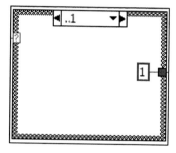

6. On the front panel, connect the icon terminals.

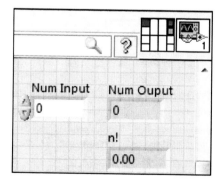

7. After we have finished creating the functions, we will start building the DLL. In the project, right-click on **Build Specifications** and build the DLL.

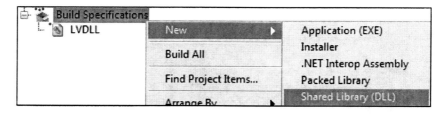

8. To set up the build, specify **Exported VIs**.

9. After we have compiled the DLL, we will try calling the functions. From the DLL, we will use the `Call Library Function` node. See the following screenshot for setting it up:

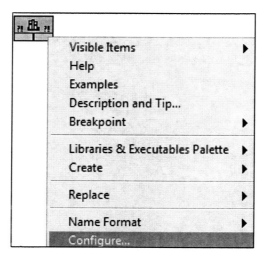

10. Within the configuration, set up each input and output required for the functions. See the following screenshot:

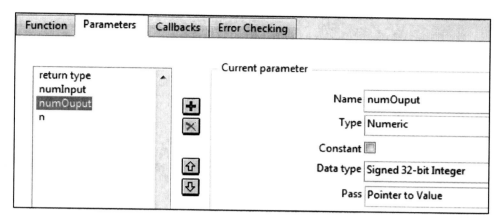

11. Wire the input and output for the node.

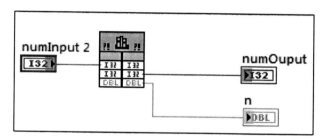

12. The `Call Library Function` node can be configured manually as described, or it can be done automatically. With the DLL and corresponding header file, we can navigate to **Tool | Import | Shared Library (.dll)** to import the DLL into VI, as shown in the following screenshot:

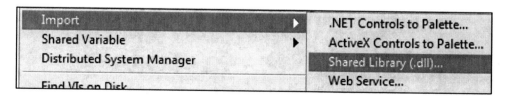

How it works...

In this example, we created a DLL with two functions, a function that takes the square of an input value, and a function that calculates the factorial of the input with two methods. The functions within the DLL are called with the `Call Library Function` node, which is set up either manually or through the import function.

A DLL allows multiple platform access. For example, a DLL can be generated in LabVIEW code and used in a C program. Also, a DLL provides a measure of security, since no one can examine the code used to compile the DLL.

Using a .NET DLL

Calling a **.NET** DLL is different than calling a C-based DLL in LabVIEW. In this example, we will demonstrate how to call functions in .NET DLL for .NET framework 4.

How to do it...

We will start by using a `BinarySearch` method of the `Array` class. In order to work with .NET DLL based on framework 4 and above, we have to create a configuration file.

1. In order to use .NET DLL based on framework 4, the `LabVIEW.exe.config` file needs to be created with content shown in the following screenshot. The file needs to be placed in the same LabVIEW folder where `LabVIEW.exe` is located, inside the LabVIEW installation folder.

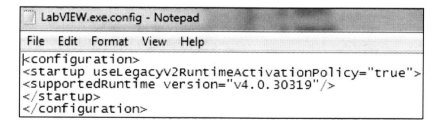

2. After the configuration file is created, the code in the following block diagram searches for the number **5** in the array [**1,4,5,5,6**] starting from index **0** and outputs its index if found. For input parameters that are .NET objects, LabVIEW data types are converted into .NET object and cast into a more specific class. To obtain the correct specific class reference, simply right-click on the input of the `Invoke Node`, and create a constant. The method called is static, so the constructor node is not needed.

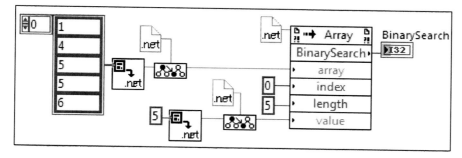

3. To select the method in the preceding diagram, see the following screenshot:

✓ [S]BinarySearch(Array array, Int32 index, Int32 length, Object value)
[S]BinarySearch(Array array, Int32 index, Int32 length, Object value, IC
[S]BinarySearch(Array array, Object value)
[S]BinarySearch(Array array, Object value, IComparer comparer)

4. The code, in the following block diagram, overwrites the destination array with the source array. For input parameters that are .NET objects, LabVIEW data types are converted into. NET object, and cast into a more specific class. To obtain the correct specific class reference, simply right-click on the input of the `Invoke Node` and create a constant. The method called is static, so constructor node is not needed. The `Invoke Node` doesn't have an output terminal. The destination array object transform from an input to an output after the method is executed. Connecting the error terminal is critical to ensure the correct sequence of execution. After the method is executed, the object is converted back to an array and outputted.

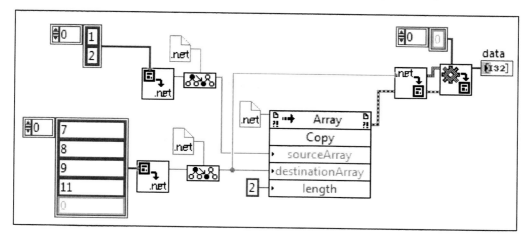

5. To select the method in the preceding block diagram, see the following screenshot:

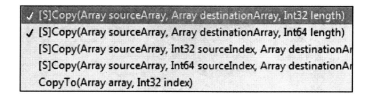

6. Previous steps involves calling static methods. We will not turn our attention to the constructor node for method that require object instantiation. The code in the following block diagram creates a string object with elements **65** and **66** in Unicode (represent character A and B respectively). The object is converted back to a variant.

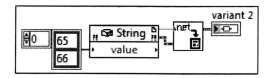

7. To select constructor, right-click on constructor and select the **String** object, as shown in the following screenshot:

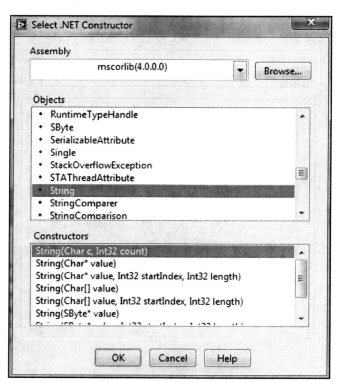

8. The code in the following block diagram creates a **String** object with elements **65** and **66** in Unicode. With the string object, the **Contains** method is invoked to determine if it does contain the character B.

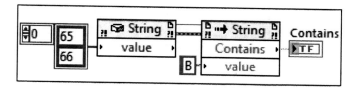

9. To select the `Contains` method, refer to the following screenshot:

10. The code in the following block diagram creates a string object with elements **65** and **66** in Unicode. With the **String** object, the **Length** property is called to determine how many characters the string has.

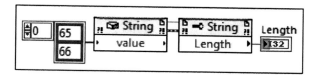

11. To select the **Length** property, refer to the following screenshot:

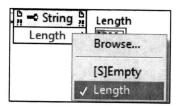

How it works...

In this example, we demonstrate how to use a .NET DLL based on framework 4 and above. To call static methods and properties, a constructor node is not needed. Otherwise, a constructor node is needed to create an object before a method or a property can be accessed. For some input/output of a .NET DLL, its data type could be an object, which needs to be created before being sent into the DLL call.

Debugging a .NET DLL

Sometimes, a DLL may have a bug that will only show up when it is called in LabVIEW. To debug such problem, LabVIEW and Microsoft Visual Studio can be used together for investigation. In this recipe, we will demonstrate how to use Microsoft Visual Studio to step through a DLL that LabVIEW is currently accessing.

How to do it...

In order to debug a .NET DLL, using Microsoft Visual Studio, we need to execute the following steps:

1. Everything including the DLL and its source code must be in a Visual Studio project. See the following screenshot for the source code of our example in C#. It contains a class called `Monsters` with `Name` and `Height` as its properties; and `Greeting` as a method.

```csharp
using System;
using System.Collections.Generic;
using System.Linq;
using System.Text;

namespace ClassExample
{
    public class Monsters
    {
        public string Name;
        public double Height;
        public string Greeting()
        {
            return @"My name is " + Name + ", and I am " + Height +
                " feet tall.  I would like to have you for lunch.  ahhhhhh!!!";
        }
    }
}
```

2. Within Visual Studio, navigate to **Build | Configuration Manager**.

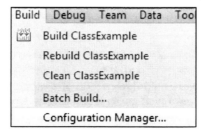

3. Within the **Configuration Manager** dialog box, confirm that the DLL is going to be complied in debug mode.

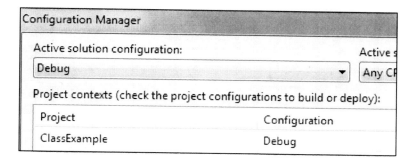

4. Build the following state machine that will call the DLL. It starts in the **Input** state to wait for the user to click on **Appear Button**. Once the button is clicked on, the program enters the **Create Monster 1** state.

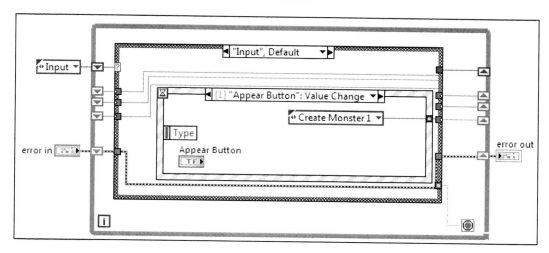

5. To exit the program, the user simply has to close the front panel.

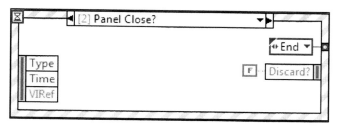

6. The next state is **"Create Monster 1"**. It uses a constructor to create a `Monsters` object. The properties of the object `Height` and `Name` are set to `3` and `Jason`.

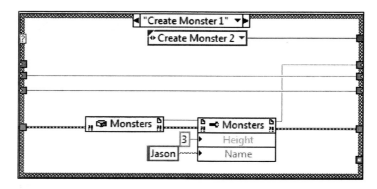

7. The next state is **"Create Monster 2"**. It creates another object with `Name` as `Johnny` and `Height` as `44`.

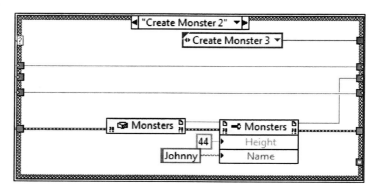

8. The next state is **"Create Monster 3"**. It creates another `Monsters` object, and set its `Height` and `Name` properties to `35` and `Billy`, respectively.

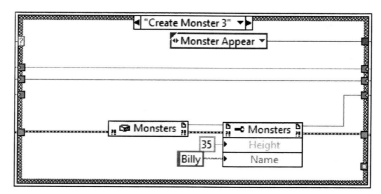

9. The next state is **"Monster Appear"**. It generates a random number between 0 to 100, and picks one of the three `Monsters` objects created based on the number. After an object is selected, its `Greeting` method is invoked with its string displayed in an indicator. Finally, it goes back to the **Input** state to wait for the user input.

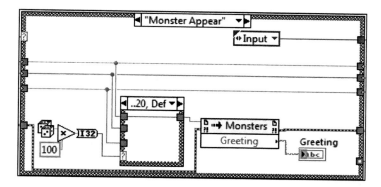

10. When user closes the front panel to exit the program, the **"End"** state is entered. The state closes the references of all objects created.

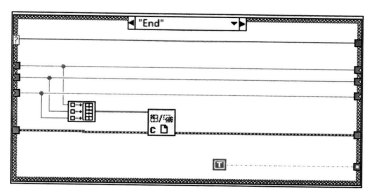

11. Include all VI and DLL in a project. If the DLL is not included, a VI will not be able to access it.

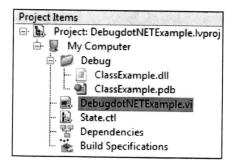

12. With DLL source code opened in Microsoft Visual Studio and DLL caller code opened in LabVIEW, in Visual Studio navigate to **Tools | Attach to Process**.

13. In the **Attach to Process** dialog, select the **LabVIEW.exe** process. The following screenshot shows the dialog with the **Qualifier** field blacked out, which is the name of the computer in which the process is running. After that, place a break point in the source code of the DLL and run the LabVIEW code. When the execution arrives at the break point, we can proceed to step through the source code of the DLL.

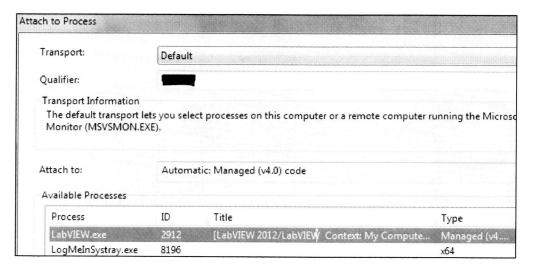

How it works...

When calling a .NET DLL in LabVIEW, with the DLL's source code opened in Microsoft Visual Studio, we can step through the code within the DLL. In the example, we created a `Monsters` class with the `Name` and `Height` properties; and a `Greeting` method. The LabVIEW code uses DLL to create three `Monsters` objects, and execute the method for one of the object at random. If there is a problem and we suspect that the DLL has a bug, we can use the method described previously to step through the source code that created the DLL one line at a time.

Using a C-based DLL

Codes can be shared through DLL. There are many DLL built-in to the window operating system. In this example, we will demonstrate how to access the built-in DLL for Windows.

How to do it...

We will create a program that can access C-based DLL in a loop:

1. Build the following block diagram. It has two loops. The top loop contains a case structure that executes the `GetSystemPowerStatus` function within the `kernel32.dll`. The bottom loop executes the `Beep` function within `kernel32.dll` with frequency and duration input set to `100` ms.

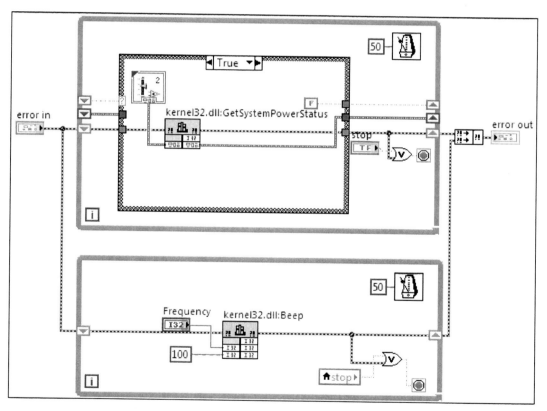

2. The input cluster for the GetSystemPowerStatus function is shown in the following screenshot:

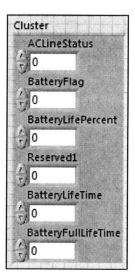

3. The **False** case of the loop is shown in the following screenshot. It displays the battery life percentage in an indicator.

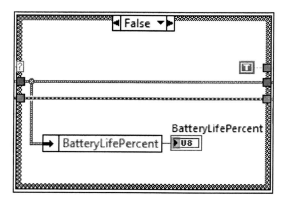

4. To set up the Call Library Function node for the GetSystemPowerStatus function within the kernel32.dll, see the following screenshot. The **Run in UI thread** is selected. Under this option, the Call Library Function node will leave the thread that it is currently using and go to the user interface thread. If the **Run in any thread** option is selected, the Call Library node can run in multiple threads, so make sure that the function node is capable of being called by multiple threads simultaneously.

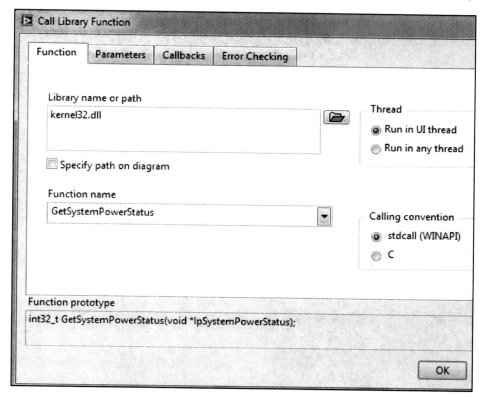

5. To set up the output, see the following screenshot:

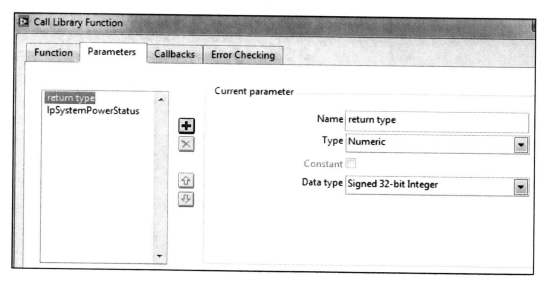

6. To set up the input, see the following screenshot:

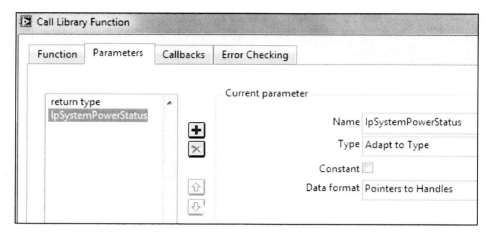

7. To set up the Beep function within the kernel32.dll, see the following screenshot:

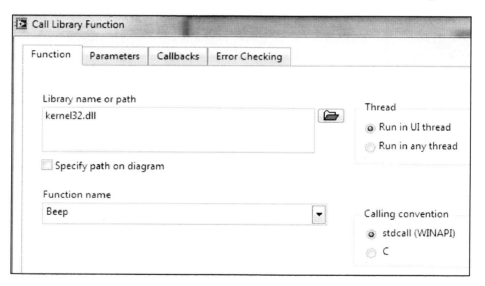

How it works...

The C-based DLL that are built-in to the Windows operating system allow the user to access functions that interact with the PC. In this example, we demonstrate how to use functions in kernel32.dll to look at the laptop battery level and output a beep tone at user-specified frequency.

Using ActiveX

ActiveX allows information sharing among different applications. In this example, we will demonstrate how to use ActiveX in LabVIEW to access the functionality of the Microsoft Excel application. In this recipe, we will create a LabVIEW program that would create a workbook, and enter a value in a user specified cell through ActiveX.

How to do it...

We will create a program that works with Excel through ActiveX.

1. Create the state machine in the following block diagram. It starts in the **User** state. In that state, when the **Run Button** is clicked on, the program would go to the **Open Excel, Add Workbook**, or **Get Worksheet** state depending on what excel reference is available.

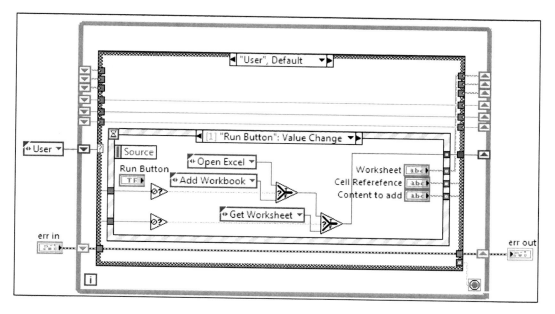

2. The next state is **"Open Excel"**. It opens the excel application and gets the required references for the next state.

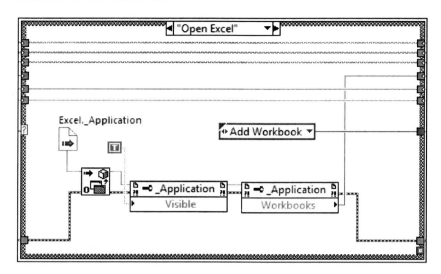

3. The next state is **"Add Workbook"**. It creates a workbook in the excel application and gets the required references for the next state. See the following diagram.

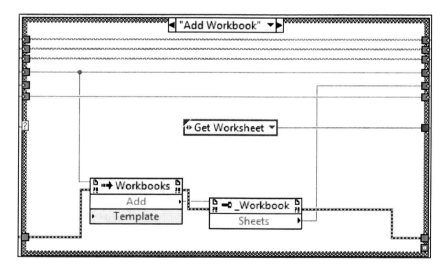

4. The next state is **"Get Worksheet"**. It gets the reference of the specified worksheet.

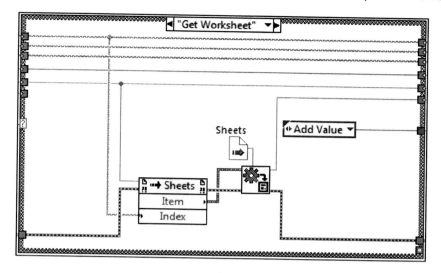

5. The next state is **"Add Value"**. It modifies the value of the specified cell.

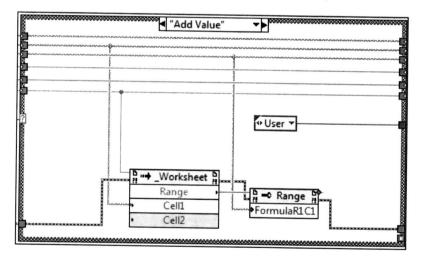

6. The last state is **"Exit"**. It sets the stop condition of the state machine to `true`.

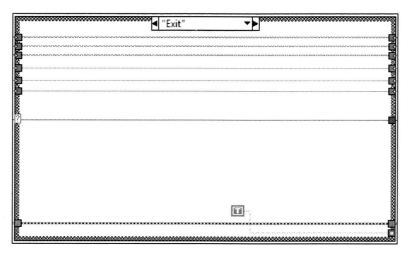

7. When opening the ActiveX session, select the object specified in the following screenshot:

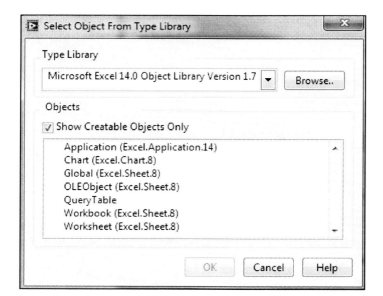

8. See the following screenshot of the front panel. The user enters the **Worksheet** label, **Cell Reference** (column and row), and **Content to add** for the cell. After all fields are populated, the user has to click on **Run** to execute the program.

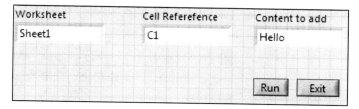

How it works...

This example interacts with the excel application by opening excel, creating a workbook, and writing a string in a cell with user-specified location. The example uses ActiveX to access the excel functionality in LabVIEW. ActiveX can also be used for other application as well such as Word, PowerPoint, and Outlook.

Building a web service

Web Service allows communication between application through the Internet. In this recipe, we will demonstrate how to build a web service in LabVIEW.

How to do it...

We will start by creating a web service that outputs a string from a string array at random.

1. Build the following block diagram. It selects an element from the string array randomly and gives the outputs.

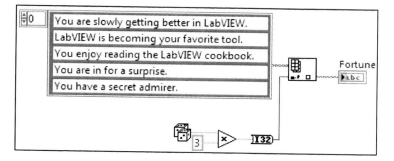

2. Build the web service in the project by navigating to **Build Specifications | New | Web Service (RESTfull)**, see the following screenshot:

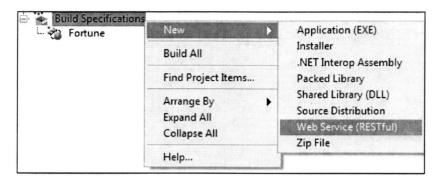

3. Set up the web service, as shown in the following screenshot:

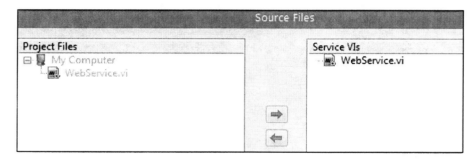

4. After the web service is compiled, deploy it. The web service is now running in the local PC.

5. To access the web service, open an Internet browser. In the address bar, enter this URL: `http://localhost:8080/Fortune/Webservice`. **Fortune** is the service name, and **Webservice** is the VI name. They are set up under the properties of **Build Specifications**. Other application can now access the web service through a web browser. The output is encoded in XML.

How it works...

In this recipe, we created a VI that outputs a string at random, like a fortune cookie. After it has been compiled into a web service and deployed, anyone can access the functionality of the web service through the Internet given the appropriate access.

Using SMTP to send e-mail

Simple Mail Transfer Protocol (**SMTP**) is a standard to send e-mails. In this recipe, we will use SMTP to send e-mail through a Gmail account.

How to do it...

We will build our e-mailing application based on a state machine architecture.

1. Build the state machine as shown in the following screenshot. It starts in the **User Input** state, and waits for the user to enter all required information and click on **Send**.

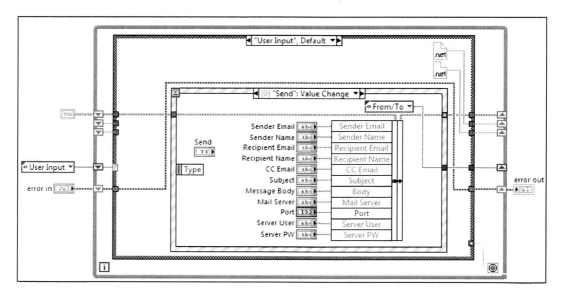

2. If the **Exit** button is clicked on, the state machine will go to the shutdown state.

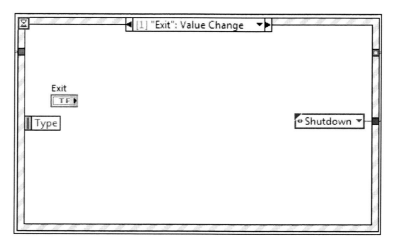

3. The next state is **"From/To"**. It creates the `MailAddress` object and sets it properties, as shown in the following screenshot:

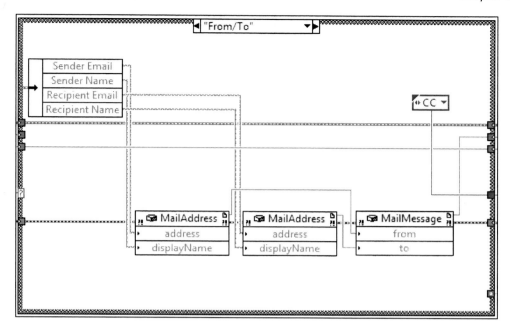

4. The next state is **"CC"**. It adds the e-mail address for the carbon copy field of the e-mail.

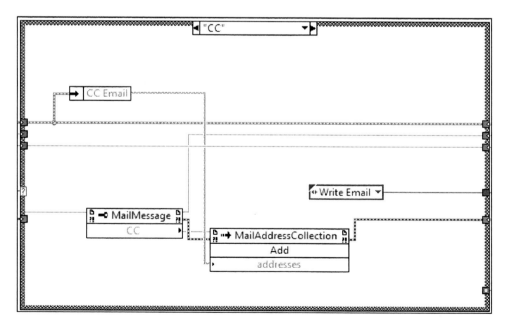

5. The next state is **"Write Email"**. It sets the subject and content of the e-mail.

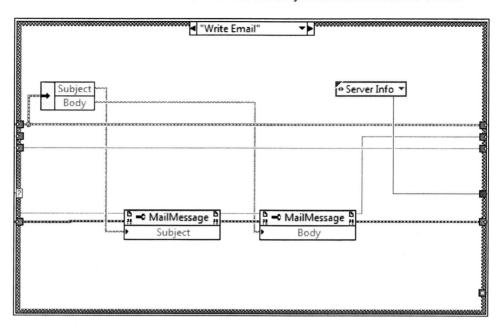

6. The next state is **"Server Info"**. It sets up the `SmtpClient` object for logging on the Gmail account.

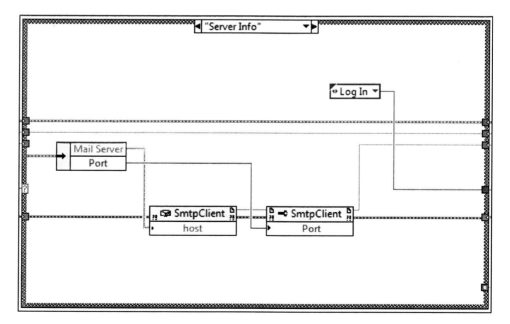

7. The next state is **"Log In"**. It uses the specified username and password to log into the Gmail server.

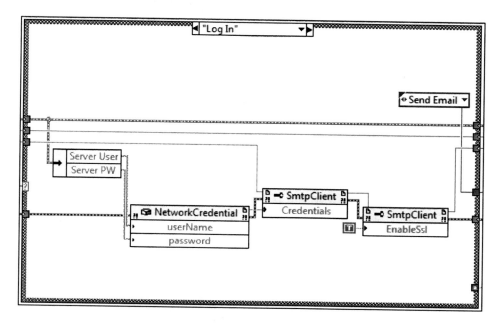

8. The next state is **"Send Email"**. It sends the e-mail out to the recipient.

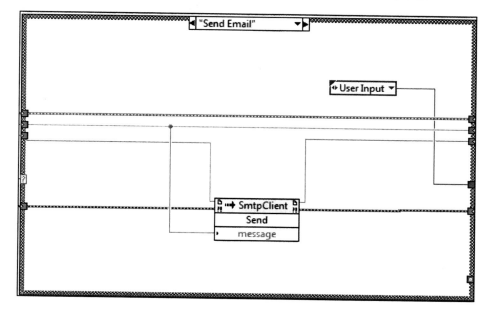

9. The last state is **"Shutdown"**. It sets the stop condition of the state machine to `true`.

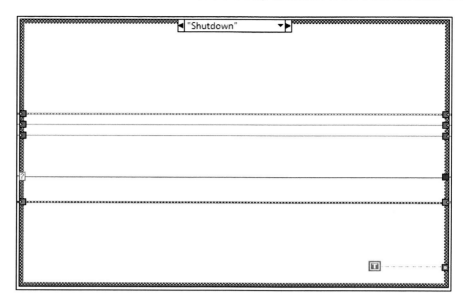

10. The front panel of the program is shown in the following screenshot. It contains information that is required to log into the Gmail server.

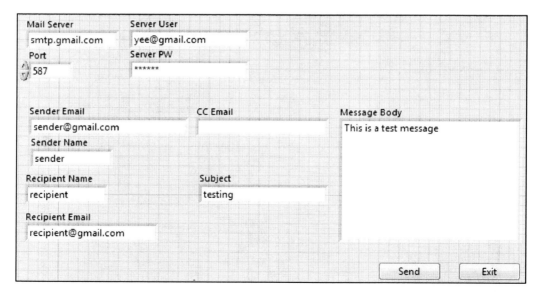

How it works...

This example sends an e-mail out to a recipient through the Gmail server with SMTP. It uses a built-in .NET DLL to accomplish such task. After the user composes an e-mail through the front panel and clicks on start, the program sets up the SMTP objects, log into the Gmail server, and then send the e-mail.

Index

Thank you for buying
LabVIEW Graphical Programming Cookbook

About Packt Publishing

Packt, pronounced 'packed', published its first book "*Mastering phpMyAdmin for Effective MySQL Management*" in April 2004 and subsequently continued to specialize in publishing highly focused books on specific technologies and solutions.

Our books and publications share the experiences of your fellow IT professionals in adapting and customizing today's systems, applications, and frameworks. Our solution-based books give you the knowledge and power to customize the software and technologies you're using to get the job done. Packt books are more specific and less general than the IT books you have seen in the past. Our unique business model allows us to bring you more focused information, giving you more of what you need to know, and less of what you don't.

Packt is a modern, yet unique publishing company, which focuses on producing quality, cutting-edge books for communities of developers, administrators, and newbies alike. For more information, please visit our website: www.PacktPub.com.

About Packt Enterprise

In 2010, Packt launched two new brands, Packt Enterprise and Packt Open Source, in order to continue its focus on specialization. This book is part of the Packt Enterprise brand, home to books published on enterprise software – software created by major vendors, including (but not limited to) IBM, Microsoft and Oracle, often for use in other corporations. Its titles will offer information relevant to a range of users of this software, including administrators, developers, architects, and end users.

Writing for Packt

We welcome all inquiries from people who are interested in authoring. Book proposals should be sent to author@packtpub.com. If your book idea is still at an early stage and you would like to discuss it first before writing a formal book proposal, contact us; one of our commissioning editors will get in touch with you.

We're not just looking for published authors; if you have strong technical skills but no writing experience, our experienced editors can help you develop a writing career, or simply get some additional reward for your expertise.

Netduino Home Automation Projects

ISBN: 978-1-84969-782-8   Paperback: 108 pages

Automate your house, save lives, and survive the apocalyse with .NET on a Netduino!

1. Automate your house using Netduino and a bunch of common components

2. Learn the fundamentals of Netduino to implement them in almost any project

3. Create cool projects ranging from self-watering plants to a homemade breathalyzer

MATLAB Graphics and Data Visualization Cookbook

ISBN: 978-1-84969-316-5   Paperback: 284 pages

Tell data stories with compelling graphics using this collection of data visualization recipes

1. Collection of data visualization recipes with functionalized versions of common tasks for easy integration into your data analysis workflow

2. Recipes cross-referenced with MATLAB product pages and MATLAB Central File Exchange resources for improved coverage

3. Includes hand created indices to find exactly what you need, such as application driven or functionality driven solutions

Please check **www.PacktPub.com** for information on our titles

Image Processing with ImageJ

ISBN: 978-1-78328-395-8   Paperback: 140 pages

Discover the incredible possibilities of ImageJ, from basic image processing to macro and plugin development

1. Learn how to process digital images using ImageJ and deal with a variety of formats and dimensions, including 4D images

2. Understand what histograms, region of interest, or filtering means and how to analyze images easily with these tools

3. Packed with practical examples and real images, with step-by-step instructions and sample code

Raspberry Pi Home Automation with Arduino

ISBN: 978-1-84969-586-2   Paperback: 176 pages

Automate your home with a set of exciting projects for the Raspberry Pi!

1. Learn how to dynamically adjust your living environment with detailed step-by-step examples

2. Discover how you can utilize the combined power of the Raspberry Pi and Arduino for your own projects

3. Revolutionize the way you interact with your home on a daily basis

Please check **www.PacktPub.com** for information on our titles

CPSIA information can be obtained at www.ICGtesting.com
Printed in the USA
LVOW05s2246120814

398869LV00005B/91/P